Poole Cen
Dolphin
Poole B
Tel: 01202 262421

D0297109

FOR SALE
WITHDRAWN
FROM STOCK

- Please return to any Libraries West
  Library by the due date.

- Renewals can be made in any
  BCP Council Library, by telephone,
  email, or online via the website.

BCP
Council

Borough of Poole Libraries

551366524 .

The Breath
of Sadness

The Breath of Sadness

Ian Ridley

On love,
grief and
cricket

Floodlit
Dreams

Published by Floodlit Dreams Ltd, 2020

Copyright © Ian Ridley, 2020

Ian Ridley has asserted his rights under the
Copyright, Design and Patents Act of 1988 to
be identified as the author of this work.

All rights reserved. No part of this publication may be
reproduced, stored in a retrieval system or transmitted in any
form or by any means electronic, mechanical, photocopying,
recording or otherwise, without the prior permission of both
the copyright owner and the above publisher of this book.

A CIP catalogue record for this book is available
from the British Library.

ISBN: 978-1-8380300-0-1

Floodlit Dreams Ltd
5–6 George St
St Albans
Herts
United Kingdom
AL3 4ER

www.floodlitdreams.com

Cover design by Steve Leard

Printed through SS Media Ltd, Rickmansworth,
Hertfordshire, WD3 1RE

Designed and set by seagulls.net

For Vikki, who else?
The maiden who bowled me over.

Ian Ridley
@IanRidley1

My beloved, bright, brilliant wife Vikki Orvice passed away at 5am, able to defy the cancer no longer. I am bereft, empty, but grateful for her life and her love. Those who feel the breath of sadness, sit down next to me.

8:58 AM - 6 Feb 2019

761 Retweets **20,865** Likes

1.5K   761   21K

Contents

Introduction

· · · · · · · · · · · · · · · · · ·

They say that writing is therapeutic, that the process of unburdening oneself can soothe the soul and quell the mind's racing. I'm dubious about that. As a professional writer, I've always thought that the process of writing, once it began after the agonies of procrastination, was plain hard work. Even painful a lot of the time.

Who, after all, am I to argue with George Orwell? "Writing a book is a horrible, exhausting struggle, like a long bout of some painful illness," he wrote. "One would never undertake such a thing if one were not driven on by some demon whom one can neither resist nor understand."

To me, it feels that if you're doing it properly and are making yourself open to feeling the words by which you seek to do justice to what you're experiencing, then as well as awakening some personal demon, you are disturbing myriad ghosts. And they seem to come out to play in those desperate hours just before fitful sleep through exhaustion, or in the wakeful panic before dawn.

Of course, there are moments when the words flow and the process becomes momentarily satisfying. More often, though, if anyone asks me if I enjoy writing, the words of Dorothy Parker come to mind. "I hate writing," she said. "I enjoy having written."

So why do it, people who do not write will inevitably ask, if it causes you so much soul-searching and heartache? Is the fleeting end really worth the prolonged means? The answer is that the elusive feeling of satisfaction, of the itch having been scratched, is the goal and the main reason why that daily resistance to starting is worth overcoming. That and the satisfaction of having something to show for the pain; the satisfaction, too, of creating something that might engage, exercise and even encourage others. Besides, ultimately, there is simply no choice. If it is a calling, it is what one does.

In the months after my bright and beloved wife Vikki Orvice – a pioneering, noted sports journalist – died of cancer on 6 February aged just 56, I simply could not write; at least, nothing comprising coherent sentences. My attention span was short. I had no stomach for adding the agony of writing to the depth of my loss and the intensity of my grief. Besides, I believed I needed to feel that grief if I was ever to get through it, not divert or distract myself from it. Life has taught me that there is no way around anything. Only through it. If you're going through hell, the saying goes, keep going.

The only thing I could do in those raw months was make abbreviated notes, to try and record, and thus make sense of, the random thoughts and feelings that swirled around my fevered brain. Vikki and I used to note occasionally – and always smile at – the story of the screenwriter Nora Ephron at her dying mother's bedside as her mother Phoebe, a writer herself, insisted: "Take notes. Everything is copy."

(And V would enjoy it that, just a page or two in, I've already quoted two women she so admired in Parker and Ephron.)

But notes were one thing, writing them up subsequently quite another. *Is* everything copy anyway? I had no stomach for stringing these thoughts into sentences, paragraphs and chapters. Why heap pain upon pain? If I wasn't going to write, though, what could I do, to borrow a pertinent phrase from the song "Leftover Wine" by Melanie, in the alone of my time?

Something did occur to me.

I had always promised myself that one year, when time opened up, perhaps through retirement when I no longer needed to chase a living, I would spend a summer watching county cricket. The comfortable vision was that in my dotage, I would be able to sit there in quiet contemplation against a backdrop of slowly unfolding action. It conjured up idyllic visions of a season in the sun. Of musing on the nature of life and my past, finding answers and peace. Of wondering, as Marlon Brando put it in his latter days, what the hell that was all about.

Then, when I was going through a particularly difficult time in the six weeks after Vikki's funeral, something my therapist said confirmed to me that watching cricket might be no bad thing.

I had been enduring a period of depression and panic attacks, brought on by suicidally dark thoughts about the worth of a future without Vikki and over regrets about the past. About things said and done, yes, but more about things left unsaid and undone. About things I had discovered in old diaries and photographs belonging to Vikki that triggered all manner of fears and insecurities in me. And about my own secondary cancer deciding, on top of everything else, that this might be a good time to remind me of its presence.

"I'm not sure," I said to that therapist, Bruce, "how long I can keep feeling this pain." (The label "therapist", by the way, doesn't begin to do him justice; this maverick operator was the man who had saved my life, on an emotional level, many times in the past 25 years after I had first gone to see him five years into my sobriety as an alcoholic who had quit drinking, having hit a wall of "Is this it?" gloom in recovery.)

"Give it the cricket season," he suggested. "See how you feel at the end of that."

We both loved the game. He had a son who had played for Hampshire county age-group teams. I had been coached properly at school, played it to a decent, and serious, club level for a dozen years – as an opening batsman too prone to nervousness – until my children were born and it became too indulgent and lengthy a pastime at weekends.

I had covered it occasionally for the newspaper I worked for in the 1980s, *The Guardian*, before realising that to do so full time did not square with having young children. For correspondents, it was an endless summer all right, but it had the potential to burn you. I didn't want familiarity to breed a contempt for the game.

In my forties, more able to handle my nerves and with the kids grown up, I made a brief playing comeback with the odd game for my then newspaper, *The Observer*. Shortly after I had met Vikki, I made a half-century against a village team in Berkshire. I can still picture V sitting on a rug, reading the Sunday papers as she loved to do, and her greeting my return to the pavilion after I was out with: "Not bad for a non-Yorkshireman." It was a proud moment. For V, that was some compliment.

Sheffield-born, Vikki enjoyed the game too. Or rather followed Yorkshire. The two aren't quite the same, given the politics and personalities of the county down the years. Indeed, her father Fred insisted that her mother Jean give birth in Sheffield, at Jessop's maternity hospital, rather than in Chesterfield, which was slightly nearer to their home on the Derbyshire border of the city's southern suburb, in case she was a boy and would thus qualify to play for the county under the eligibility rules that existed back then in 1962.

We had been a few times to 20-overs-a-side games to watch Yorkshire, at Leicester and Northampton, and she was most excited by the short form of the game. We were planning that winter before her illness overcame her to travel to the West Indies to watch England play a Test match. She was willing to indulge my preference for the rhythm and cadences of the longer form of the game since sunshine trumped tedium for her.

The summer of 2019 would prove to be the saddest of my life but one of the most joyous in the history of English cricket. There would be a thrilling 50-over World Cup, won by the host nation in the most dramatic of fashions at Lord's. There would be a drawn Ashes series, meaning the urn was retained by Australia. It would contain one of the greatest English wins, as Ben Stokes at Headingley delivered one of the most breathtaking Test innings ever and went on to become the BBC Sports Personality of the Year, a rare accolade for a cricketer.

For me, as exciting as they were to watch on television, these were raucous, crowded events where I did not feel I belonged that summer of mourning. The appeal for me was the peace and solitude of the County Championship, at which I could explore and experience, as reflection of the "action", the rhythms and cadences of my grief. With, hopefully, the sun on my back, and tea, cake and crossword at my side.

I studied the fixtures and made a plan. I would visit places that had meant something to Vikki and me, places where we had history. There would be Hove, the Isle of Wight, Leicester and Northampton, Lord's, Scarborough and The Oval.

And so at the dawn of the season in early April, I headed for the coast. The trip came after a dark late winter and early spring of death and grief – short words but long on emotion – that comprised those five stages they talk about. But denial, anger, bargaining, depression and acceptance (this last one fleeting compared to the intensity of the others) have sub-headings that have sub-headings. Besides, you – well, I as I can only speak for myself; it varies from person to person – can go in and out of each one all in the same day, the same hour. Much of my grieving experience was random, little of it linear. I would make baby steps forward but retreat by strides the length of a fast bowler's.

It is why what follows in these pages, when I did begin to write again, is structured the way it is. Sometimes in flashbacks. In and out of moods and moments. Echoes on the wind. So much of grief, for me at least, became about events, sights and sounds triggering feelings and memories. Once I did begin to write again, I wanted to produce a work that mirrored the unpredictability of grief that could creep up stealthily, a book that discomforts and even unnerves at times, makes you wonder where you are and what is going on here, the way that grief does for those who experience it. Like grief, too, cricket has its moods, its ebbing and flowing, its lassitude and inactivity before huge waves, of emotion as well as action, carry you with it for the ride.

That I slowly began to string sentences together is due to a new media outlet called *Tortoise*, which produces "slow news" and longer reads, and I remain grateful to them for stirring me anew into action. Alerted by the volume of reaction to Vikki's death by both mainstream and social media, an editor there, Keith Blackmore, once of *The Times*, asked me if I might feel able to write 5,000 words about her, her death and us.

At first I baulked. I didn't want to bleed in public. I wasn't the first person to suffer the death of his wife, was I? But I slowly came to realise that what happened to me after Vikki died, particularly in the resurfacing of my own personal insecurities deriving from events in my past that collided with my very present grief, seemed to be discussed very little. I could relate to the sadness of many works about grief, but only in Joan Didion's book *The Year of Magical Thinking* about the death of her husband and her frantic year afterwards, did I connect with the madness that it can provoke. And I can't deny that that is what happened to and with me.

Toni Morrison, that most quotable of writers, once said: "We die. That may be the meaning of life. But we do language. That may be the measure of our lives." And – most pertinently – "If there is a book you want to read, but it hasn't been written yet, then you must be the one to write it."

Well, I hadn't read a book about how somebody turned to the power of sport, cricket in particular, to try and make some sense of what had happened and what I was going through. I also checked it out with Bruce. "You should turn your wounds into wisdom," he said.

And so, pondering all this, I came round to the idea of the article, which would appear on the *Tortoise* website as well as in a quarterly book they published. Keith's sensitivity also helped me a great deal in the process. Besides, Vikki should be commemorated by the person who knew her best, loved her most, I felt. And she always told me to be honest about her and us.

The reaction to the piece was heartening, from people who were simply touched to those who said it had helped them in their own grief, and all the more so when *The Sunday Times* then published an edited version of it. That reaction became the catalyst for this book.

I once read some advice to a writer that echoed the words of Nora Ephron's mother: "Every scar has a story. Tell it."

These are my scars. This is my – make that *our* – story.

· I ·

#GOSBTS

Good old Sussex by the sea, or #GOSBTS as its short-hand on Twitter has it these days, seemed like a good place to start my summer. Hove actually, as the name of a shop on Western Avenue not far from the County Ground had it. They were playing Leicestershire and the fixture had resonance for both Vikki and me.

I'd kept a one-bedroomed flat near the cricket ground for a few years and would go there for a couple of days a week, or longer if Vikki was away on a work trip covering athletics in her capacity as athletics correspondent of *The Sun*, to write whatever project I had on the go. Sometimes, I would nip across to the ground to catch the last couple of hours after tea if I'd had a productive day at the laptop.

Leicester, meanwhile, was where Vikki had gone to university and earned a good degree in English. Those who joked about the literacy skills of *Sun* reporters did not know her. She was a lovely writer, given half a chance. She could have written for any paper, broadsheet or tabloid. Could have written creatively. I knew that better than anyone, and would discover again a month or so after her funeral when I came to examine the contents of her office at home into which I had rarely ventured when she was alive.

I thought the sea air would do me good. A short early-spring holiday, a long weekend, that first week of April when the County Championship began. A rite of the year, a reawakening, as the Masters golf on the TV also heralded. After everything, I deserved something diverting, I thought. And so I booked myself into the Holiday Inn on the Brighton seafront for four nights, which meant I could watch all four days of the match and head straight home afterwards.

I drove down the night before, leaving after the M25 had done its worst, so that I could get a good night's sleep, have a leisurely breakfast before strolling to what was now called the 1st Central (no, me neither; I googled it and it's car insurance) County Cricket Ground.

This Friday morning was bright, warmer than I had expected, but there was still a chilly edge to the wind whipping off the Channel and up the narrow streets leading north to that long east–west shopping street of Western Avenue that linked Brighton with Hove.

Once at Palmeira Square, just before the Town Hall, I turned right up Salisbury Road past all the rambling old detached town houses, most of them now turned into flats. There I encountered like-minded souls, mainly middle-aged white men and women with time on their hands, the grey pound filling their pockets, and newspapers and thermos flasks in their backpacks. They were walking a little more quickly than they might later in the season.

This was the opening day, after all. A spring was in the step and anticipation in the air.

At the gates on Eaton Road, I paid my £17 entry at the Portakabin that served as ticket office, and an extra fiver on top for access to the pavilion, which seemed to be well worth it. I picked up a coffee at Greig's (no, not Gregg's, but the cafe named after the former Sussex and England captain Tony) and found a seat on an old lacquered bench just next to the steps where the players emerged from their elevated dressing rooms. I was here in plenty of time and needn't have worried about the best spots being bagged. The start time of 11 a.m. was still half an hour away.

I have always loved Hove. It is a far cry from the big Test venues and has a low-key charm all of its own. At either end, the Sea and Cromwell Road ends, blocks of flats overlook the ground. On one side is the pavilion, with its restaurant, long room (which bears little relation to the one at Lord's and instead often smells of chips), tea bar and two-tiered seating adjacent to the one big stand in the place. On the other side, a few hospitality boxes have been erected in what is these days called "Cow Corner".

My preference is always to watch cricket from behind the bowler's arm whenever possible. Side on, you can barely see the ball when it fizzes through quickly. From an end, you can follow its flight, see whether it is swinging or turning. It is doubly delightful at Hove as they have deckchairs at the Cromwell Road end. I declined the chance today, though, recalling that the last time I had been here a couple of years previously, they were so comfortable, and the atmosphere so somnolent, that I had fallen asleep and woken to feel sunburn on my cheeks and the backs of my hands.

I didn't want to do that today, not on the first morning of the season, because I had company arriving. An old friend and colleague, Paul Hayward, elegant and perceptive chief sports writer of the *Daily Telegraph,* who had been at Vikki's funeral, lived nearby and had accepted my invitation to lunch in the pavilion restaurant.

He arrived at midday with Sussex having made the worst possible start. The first wicket went down without a run on the board and it was soon 5 for two. It was 36 for five when Paul arrived and we shook hands and smiled at renewed acquaintance. He had much to take credit for over the next few hours. First, Sussex stabilised – as he noted – under his watchful gaze. Second, he tolerated me lamenting my lot. It had been just six weeks since the funeral and everything had caught up with me in that period.

Paul listened generously as I went through my painful memories of the past year, of Vikki's cancer and her dying. I even risked talking about elements of the anxieties of these past few months, which would assail me for a while yet and that came from gaps in my knowledge about Vikki and her life. V and I were the closest people to each other but had always allowed the other an independence. Now I was alone, insecurities and ignorance were at times overwhelming me with an illogical but all too real panic that would take me many sessions with Bruce to understand.

Paul, a sensitive man, discussed his own life and experiences, offered consolation in talking of press trips abroad when he had been at sporting events with Vikki and told of how she had always talked about me excitedly, of what I was doing, what I was writing. Bless him for that day saying the right things as I sat on my emotional ledge, from where many had been trying to talk me down.

And we also talked of matters that I did not need to talk about but keenly wanted to as antidotes to the anxiety. Of newspapers and sports writing, of colleagues and old anecdotes. Of football. By mid-afternoon, he needed to go, he said. He had to prepare for tomorrow's match at Wembley – the local team Brighton and Hove Albion up against Manchester City in an FA Cup semi-final. Our few hours together had been what I needed: compassionate company on the same wavelength.

The afternoon grew cold – a two-sweater day for the players and a windcheater day for the spectators. Sussex staggered to 173 all out; Leicestershire lost quick wickets too. The wicket was green and lively and there was rustiness in the joints of these players.

I shivered with cold, wondering about the wisdom of all this. The County Championship was sponsored by Specsavers but it wasn't my eyes that needed testing. I decided to go inside for tea and cake and to watch from the warmth of the long room. Others had the same idea. As I look back now, it sounds fun, even idyllic, notwithstanding the inevitable chill at this time of year, although global warning did seem to have made that less predictable in recent years when April, far from being the cruellest month of T.S. Eliot, could be ablaze.

Sounds fun but wasn't. No matter how charming the circumstances, how pleasing the external views, if the prospect and the feelings within are dark, there can be no idyll. Environment can offer comfort but sometimes you just can't persuade your insides to reflect what's going on outside.

I grew restless, agitated. I had been away from home for the odd couple of nights here and there to stay with good friends at their homes but never on my own, in a hotel, before now. I couldn't sit still for too much longer and so, some 30 minutes before the close, I retraced my steps to the hotel. Having had a roast lunch with Paul in the pavilion, I just picked up a sandwich on the way.

Back in my hotel room, I tried to read, watch TV, do anything, but it was a restless, anxious 16 hours or so before it was time to go back to the cricket. I had slept reasonably well on the first night – that is to say, in keeping with my usual pattern by now of a couple of hours' sleep followed by two awake, mind racing, through the night. Tonight, though, it was a night for watching news channels until their loops became tiresome and hoping the World Service wasn't at its tedious worst. I couldn't work out if taking framed pictures of Vikki to place around the room had been a good or bad idea.

Come the morning, surely the cricket, with its gentle pace, would soothe this edginess, the state that had become familiar since Vikki's funeral? Surely the few hours with Paul yesterday were not mere respite while my mind was occupied by someone else's conversation? For a few hours at least, I had felt some hope for the first time in a while. Today, however, marked two months since Vikki's death. What was I even doing here? I should be at home, in our house, contemplating the occasion.

The ground was more sparsely populated than yesterday, which surprised me at first until I recalled that pretty much the whole of Sussex would be decamping during the day to Wembley for the FA Cup semi-final. It was a shame not only because the game was finely balanced but also because – something I overheard two Sussex supporters discussing – this would be the only Saturday County Championship day's play of the whole summer at Hove. How sad that sounded for this competition once central to the British sporting calendar.

Now, this was to be a busy summer, fitting in the domestic one-day 50-over competition early so that the World Cup could have centre stage, but there had to be something wrong with a timetable that had so little four-day cricket at the height of summer. The schedule this season told of a splurge early on and late in September with little in between. To this aficionado, rekindling his love for the game rather than familiar with the intricacies of its politics these days, it seemed scarcely designed to develop and improve potential Test cricketers.

It would be interesting to see how it all fitted together, and what effect it might have, as England chased a first one-day World Cup title later this summer then went straight into a home Ashes series. The country's cricketing authorities were also, it appeared to me as I reacquainted myself with the game, chasing the cash that came more readily through the one-day game, in both its 50- and 20-over versions. Then again, that sounded understandable if it subsidised the four-day game. I decided to ponder that as a diversion, but it would have to be examined at another time, when I had seen more cricket, knew more. For now, more pressing concerns were never far from assailing me.

I had begun yesterday enjoying my circumstances and surroundings as a break from my morning, and mourning, routine. Today much rankled. Spectators were talking too loudly nearby, not settling to watch the cricket. Players were shouting, more than I ever recalled them doing, applauding the most average of balls, clapping hands like seals. I shouldn't be here among people. I should be on my own, honouring the day, the sixth of the month.

As the day wore on and Leicestershire recovered from their own poor start to build a healthy lead, I grew ever more distracted, unable to concentrate. Visions of Vikki rarely left me, along with dark thoughts and feelings that I'd been experiencing due to those discoveries of photos and diaries in filing cabinets and drawers at home. They shouldn't really have upset me yet they had led me, disturbingly, in dubious directions I was not expecting and to this raw state.

I stayed as long as I could at the game, moving seats several times as I was uncomfortable, not so much with the benches as myself. At least that was something: I wasn't stuck in one allocated seat all day as I could be at bigger sporting events. This freedom was precisely why I wanted to try days at the county game. A huge part of me wanted to go back to the hotel room, to shut myself away in isolation again, to experience my panicking in private, but it would have been to have given in. I needed to stick it out, I decided.

I did, at least until I realised I could get back and watch the Brighton match on TV. That would occupy my mind. I didn't have to force myself to endure this if I didn't want to, did I? I was at liberty to choose. And people kept telling me there was no right or wrong in my condition;

that I just had to take care of myself. But I wasn't used to any of that, of just looking after number one. I no longer had Vikki to think about and I hated it. I would have given anything to have had my freedom taken away by preoccupying myself with her and her illness now.

I walked briskly back to the hotel, settled in, ordered a room-service curry and tried to tell myself that I was lucky. Lucky to be watching county cricket. Lucky to be able to afford a hotel and room service. Lucky to be a man of leisure these days, if I so chose. After all, I had pensions and legacies following Vikki's death and I couldn't deny that they took the pressure off me. "Never believe anyone who tells you the money doesn't help," a friend who had inherited money from her mother had said to me, and I could only agree. Why, though, did I not feel lucky? No second guesses needed, really.

Soon there were sounds of people running along the corridor outside my room. They were laughing, joking, shouting. Women's voices mainly. I opened my door and looked out. They were heading for somewhere just round the corner from my room. Frocked-up and barefoot, they were carrying bottles of prosecco and flute glasses. And just round the corner was a large room containing tables decorated with balloons and groaning under bottles. No more than 10 yards from my room, around a dozen women were clearly preparing for a hen night.

I could also hear noise from the reception area below and so I made my way downstairs. It was thronged with young people, men in their uniform of short-sleeved shirts untucked over grey trousers, and more young women in skirts that were less mini or micro than just slightly long T-shirts. It turned out that, as well the hen party, there was also a stag do. And, to boot, the hotel was also staging an amateur boxing tournament.

I felt overwhelmed and grew panicky. I don't know why I hadn't expected it (er, Brighton: Saturday night; stag and hen dos? doh), but I needed the sanctuary of my room again, quickly. Except that it was no longer sanctuary. The noise from the hen night was rising. It was still only 8 p.m. There was no way I would be able to tolerate a night of this.

I quickly packed my bags, made my way down to reception and paid my bill, including that night's. The cost was the last thing on my mind but thankfully they didn't charge me for the cancelled night tomorrow. I hurried to my car in the car park (I always drove everywhere in case I needed to make a quick getaway) and in about 90 minutes of speeding, I was back in my own home. Back in the familiarity of Vikki. Her clothes. The growing collection of photographs of her, and us, that I'd framed. Her very presence. Despite darkness approaching and it being a Saturday, the night in the week that most made me agitated, I felt some relief.

In other times, I might have beaten myself up, considered myself an old fogey and killjoy who couldn't bear to see other people enjoying themselves. (On holiday in Italy

once, Vikki had been playfully annoyed with me that I
didn't want to go and join in with a wedding reception
downstairs that was keeping us awake when she was up
for a bop.) And it was true that right now, I couldn't bear
to watch ostentatious displays of enjoyment when I was
hurting so badly. People couldn't know they were intruding on private grief. I was intruding on private merriment.

The experience of pain had taught me to try and
accept where I was, that this was how I was just for
today. I was simply glad to be in my own comfortable,
controlled environment when so much else was out of
my control. And that feeling trumped any other. For
now. Soon some others would kick in.

I'd had visions of spending the summer travelling the
length and breadth of the country, watching four days of
county matches – weather permitting and assuming they
didn't finish before that because wickets were dodgy or
English batsmen had forgotten how to occupy the crease.
But after two long nights away, I simply couldn't wait
to be home.

It was funny – peculiar not ha, ha – that I could now
go anywhere in the world, at any time I wanted. I had
the time and no commitments. That was why I planned
to spend the summer watching cricket. Yet all I wanted
was to be in my own home. Vikki's home. Our home. It
did not bode well.

The relief was as familiar as the sadness. It was like
my body, mind and spirit were undergoing a series of

mini-breakdowns – meltdowns, in modern parlance – until my being needed a break from the intensity. Until I felt weary enough – tired of being tired – either to collapse or surrender.

But what was this? It turned into the first Saturday night for a month that I sensed anything other than panic attacks in going to bed. And through exhaustion, I slept. For five uninterrupted hours, anyway. And then... the next day was a Sunday. The second part of the weekend, and weekends had become painfully lonely and terrifying. If I thought I'd got away with it, I was mistaken. The prospect of a Sunday at home alone again became overwhelmingly frightening.

Once, I had enjoyed weekends. V and I were in a routine – we both covered football for newspapers on Saturday afternoons, then enjoyed TV dinners or takeaways on Saturday evenings. Maybe she wrote on Sunday morning while I cooked a roast. Maybe a walk in the afternoon, and a film or a detective series on a Sunday night. Those days were no more, though. The past five weekends since Vikki's funeral had been the saddest, scariest of my life and were growing in potency. I had expected to feel many things, many painful things, but I had not expected to feel all this. And it seemed to be getting worse, not better.

"This" involved stuff I just did not want to feel but I had no choice. I was – am – a recovering alcoholic, so there was no alternative but to endure the reality of it without anaesthetic. Mood-altering liquids or substances were, to me, simply not an option. My 30 years of sobriety had been too hard-won. I had long since decided that when my time came, I was going to die sober.

I now understood fellow alcoholics and addicts who shared in Twelve Step meetings about being more likely to take their own lives rather than drink or drug or gamble again. After the last six months that I'd been through with Vikki's deterioration and death, was it really any surprise that I might consider that?

· 2 ·

Cold November Rain

· ·

When does the grieving start? Is it the day of death or is it postponed until the evening after the funeral, due to preoccupation with all the arrangements that have to be made? Is it that time when everyone has gone home and the loneliness of loss bites? Or was it even long before that, in 2007, when Vikki was first diagnosed with a secondary cancer, which meant that it was incurable and everything thereafter was simply about extending life because we knew it was going to get her sooner or later? As it will me.

Perhaps – though it would have to go on hold as there was so much still to endure – my process began the day we were told that for her, the game was up.

That moment came on a dank mid-November day in 2018. We had risen at 5.30 a.m. to beat the traffic into London and secure a free parking space at the back of the Royal Marsden Hospital off the Fulham Road, a place we had both come to trust, almost love, since electing for treatment at what is an NHS hospital but a specialist, and brilliant, cancer facility. V had first come more than 11 years ago. I followed her, diagnosed with prostate cancer, two years later.

We knew it would be a long day. She was to have a blood transfusion to try and boost her body sufficiently for it to tolerate a new round of chemotherapy, which she desperately needed to interrupt the march of the cancer. These things took time. You had to be patient. Racing for free parking was less about saving £40 in meter charges and more about not having to leave the hospital every few hours to move the car and pay all over again. I wanted to be with her for the whole time.

It was, however, during a brief few moments when I wasn't with her that the drama began, one in which the last act would also be signalled.

She was on the Critical Assessment Unit, a neat, clean and well-appointed hospital ward that represents the Marsden's A&E department, though one only open by day. It was a place for those having problems with their treatment. Vikki had struggled – growing more lethargic, less mobile – through the last few months and was now struggling yet more.

She had struggled, indeed, for the whole of the last year ever since being told late in 2017 that her cancer – which had begun in early 2007 as pleurisy through fluid around the lungs during a cold winter and progressed over the next 12 years through breast, chest and back – was now in her liver. They were just, for now, "lesions", we were told. Three of them. Small, though, said the consultant.

I had always thought lesions were like small cuts but Vikki knew better. They were clusters of abnormal cells. Almost tumours, and she was wise to what that meant. "Once it's in your organs, it's the slippery slope," she'd said.

For once, she had not responded to chemotherapy. Or rather, through 2018, several chemotherapies. The side effects this time, these times, had been brutal. Her consultants would change the drugs, try new combinations, but still she lost her hair, grew weaker, struggled to walk, suffered from fatigue. And fatigue is not tiredness. Fatigue is debilitating lethargy.

By the end of August that year, she was exhausted. She had been determined to cover the World Athletics Championships in Berlin that month and, while she did it as brilliantly as ever, it had taken its toll. Her temperature was spiking at more than 40 degrees one night – dangerously high. I rang the Marsden, only to be told they had no beds and that I should take her to an A&E local to us. The Marsden rang ahead to alert them to the urgency. Meanwhile, we would be put on a list for a bed at the Marsden.

Vikki was diagnosed with sepsis and pneumonia, both life-threatening with her immune system vulnerable, and as she worsened over the next 11 days into the middle of September, bloating with all the drugs, I feared for her. Finally, I contacted the Marsden again, even begging in a long email for a bed. They clicked into action and she was transferred the next day. She wept with relief when she arrived there. "I feel like I've come home," she said between tears. I wept for and with her. After another 10 days of her regaining some strength, enough to be sent home, the crisis was averted. They would not risk the chemo on her any more, however. She was too weak to tolerate its toxicity.

Today, here on CAU this November day six weeks on from that crisis, we were desperate for the blood transfusion to work so that she could take more chemo that might just keep those lesions from graduating to tumours.

I had gone to get two cups of tea, Vikki sitting on a bed and saying she would be fine in her cubicle, curtains drawn to the side for privacy for her and those next to her. As I ambled back onto the ward, though, she was far from fine. I suddenly saw two nurses running towards her bed to assist another nurse.

Vikki was no longer on her bed but on the floor and all I could see from a few yards away was her face, more specifically her eyes. Those beautiful hazel irises were rolling in their sclera. My immediate thought, in my fearful state, was that she was having a heart attack or an anaphylactic shock. I genuinely thought she was dying.

I crumbled, fell to my knees in the middle of the ward, began to hyperventilate. The only sounds coming from my mouth were a series of loud groans. A nurse came to attend to me. She asked me my name but I couldn't answer. I just looked at her, in terror, my mouth still able only to issue loud groans. My reaction, in hindsight, was not just about what I was witnessing and fearing. It was a reaction to a year of treatment, procedures, hospital visits, consultations. And 21 days of Vikki in hospital, she laid low, me exhausted by daily visits.

Now, in the background, I could see a whole army of medics arriving and filling the cubicle; at least a dozen of them and in all manner of uniforms. They were, I would find out later, the crash team. I could see curtains being drawn around all the other cubicles on the ward. It must have been disturbing, terrifying to them too.

"It's all right," the nurse standing over me said. "She's come round."

I got myself together and finally walked over to Vikki, who was still on the floor. Her eyeballs were now fixed rather than rolling. I kissed her on the temple. "I'm here V," I said. "I'll be just a few yards away. I'm going to let these people do their jobs."

Soon she was back on the bed and I was apologising, in my shame, to the nurses, doctors and patients in neighbouring beds for my shocked reaction. I worried that if this was how I reacted now, how might I be if on my own with her and she took an even more serious turn for the worse?

It turned out that Vikki had only fainted, but she was weak, her iron levels low. They put her on a drip to pump vitamins into her. She was to have a series of tests on top of the blood transfusion.

And so I watched over the next six hours as they infused drugs and blood into her – once they had located an elusive vein in which to insert a cannula – and wheeled her away for an MRI scan. I drank tea and did the *Daily Telegraph* crossword when she wasn't there. When she was, we talked of football and work. And cancer.

The consultant came back to the ward in mid-afternoon but was clearly busy. "With you soon," she mouthed when we caught her eye. Looking back, she was putting off speaking to us. It was almost 5 p.m. when she did return, a colleague alongside her. She had that look adopted by newsreaders when the death toll is rising in a natural disaster.

"I am so sorry, Vikki," she said. "The lesions in your liver have grown and there is no more chemo we can give you for it."

There was a silence, which I didn't want to be the first to break. I held my head in my hands. Vikki shook her head.

"So basically," she said, "I'm fucked."

The consultant smiled sympathetically. I did not. I had no need to adopt the newsreader's face. I felt the shock and sadness for real.

Vikki asked calmly about any more potential treatment. There was no question of surgery, they said. The cancer was virulent. It would just spread elsewhere. They were going to put her on a tablet that might fool the disease for a while longer but we were, the consultant said, into the realm of palliative care now. I had heard the word many times down the years, knowing generally what it meant if not specifically. I soon came to learn that palliative meant relieving pain without treating the causes of an illness. In short, it meant terminal, though the word was never used. Somehow end-of-life seems less brutal.

The hits just kept on coming. V was asked about signing a non-resuscitation document, in case she lost consciousness. She was told that "resus" would be vicious, that her sternum could be broken and that she might not survive it anyway. She agreed to sign.

She also asked about whether she might go back to work. Like me, and something we had both learned from our working-class parents, V had an overdeveloped work ethic. What she did – covering football and athletics – had defined her for so long. She had always believed that carrying on, travelling, covering events, was the best way of defying the cancer.

No more. It would be wise, she was advised, to think more about things she really wanted to do now. The unspoken end to the sentence was: "While you can." I chipped in with stuff about time with family, about little trips away as treats. About enjoying the simple pleasure of good company, good food, our home. Vikki half-smiled and nodded but I could see that while she agreed in theory, in practice it felt like giving up, like second best to an active professional life.

Otherwise, I asked little, though I had much I wanted to know. Vikki hated me intruding on what was her cancer and her time with her consultants or seeking information from them in front of her. Anyway, she didn't want a detailed prognosis. Never had. When they left, I turned and looked her in the eye.

Both of us being sufferers from secondary cancer – mine having spread from my prostate after initial radiotherapy to my pelvic lymph nodes six years previously – we both knew this day would come. We didn't know who would be first and we hoped that it would be a while yet, for either of us. She, it had to be said, was odds-on, however. She had wanted us to write a book together called "My Cancer's Worse Than Yours".

"You," I said now, in a cubicle in CAU after a 10-hour day here with few other patients still around us, "have been the love of my life. Just a shame you've been so mardy at times."

"And you've been the love of my life," she replied. "Just a shame it took you so long to leave your wife."

We both smiled. We both liked a qualification, a subordinate clause. It lightened the unbearable bleakness of being. Or, today, the probability of not being.

She shed a few tears, I hugged her and held mine back, but otherwise I was astonished by the sangfroid of such a hot-blooded person. I went to get tea to go with the orange Club biscuits I had bought earlier at the Friends of the Royal Marsden cafe in Outpatients. She loved orange Club biscuits. It became a joke that I would offer one to her but not hand it over until she had sung with me the old advertising jingle: "If you like a lot of chocolate on your biscuit join our Club." I wasn't going to stop today; it was important to be normal. She smiled as I forced her to go through the ritual.

Now mobile again, she had business to take care of, she said, something administrative somewhere in the hospital. A prescription, I think. I let her go and took my opportunity. Upstairs, I found the doctor who had been alongside the consultant. She was rushing from room to room but she knew what we had just been through, saw the pain inscribed on my face, and agreed to my request for five minutes in private.

"I would like to know what I am dealing with now," I said. "How long does she have?"

"We are notoriously bad at these things," she replied, leaving me to think that she was not going to commit herself. She soon added, however: "But we are looking at months not years."

I took this in. "Eleven months? Less?"

"Less."

"Six?"

"Maybe," she said.

"OK. How will she die?"

"She'll get more and more tired, be less mobile and sleep more until she's bedridden."

"Will she be in pain?"

"She shouldn't be. Not if we manage it properly with morphine."

I nodded and thanked her and made my way in slow motion to the pharmacy on the ground floor, where Vikki was waiting for her regular assortment of drugs to take home. Noticeably this time, though, it contained fewer bottles of potions and boxes of pills that always had V joking that our medicine cabinet would put a Russian shot-putter to shame.

I smiled and she held my arm as we made our way back to the car. I cursed the London traffic, even slower in the rain, and we listened to the end of *PM*, followed by the news on Radio 4. All Brexit. She asked me to take her to see a friend, Moira, in our village. I dropped her off for an hour so she could share her news, get feedback, from a trusted third party.

Later in bed, she read a magazine, noisily flicking the pages in the way that always annoyed me – though I could not rebuke her, tonight of all nights – while I finished the crossword. We turned off the bedside lights, cuddled into each other and listened to the midnight news on the radio. More Brexit.

Everything had changed and nothing had.

I lay awake in sadness while she snored. Yes, maybe I got my first taster of grief that day but it would have to wait. I realised that I could not allow the sadness to overtake me. For her sake. There was work to be done. So much work, it would transpire.

· 3 ·

I Loves You Porgy

· ·

The steroids and the other drugs that Vikki had to take inevitably extracted their toll. She bloated, her sleep became fitful. It became hard work for her to walk, an ordeal to get up and down the stairs, made worse by her resentment of my help. Strong, independent was who she was and I reluctantly understood. Her only consolation was that her hair, which she had lost during the couple of rounds of chemo that she had tolerated earlier in the year (do they call them rounds because they resemble the punishment taken during boxing bouts?) began to grow back, albeit fuzzily. She no longer had to wear the wig she had chosen carefully in the spring to resemble her old hair and style.

I rose with her early in the morning, she wired from the steroids, that refreshing first cup of tea of the day the lure, and we sat in our dressing gowns hunting for something to watch on TV. We tired of cheesy *BBC Breakfast* and Piers Morgan on ITV – actually had never been anything less than tired of Piers Morgan – and settled on England's winter Test cricket series in Sri Lanka.

Vikki liked the fact that Joe Root was the England captain and his fellow Yorkshireman Johnny Bairstow a prominent figure. Soon we were engaged with it and began to look forward to rising early, enjoyed seeing them perform so unusually competently in the southern hemisphere that the series was won 3-0.

"Where are England playing after Christmas?" Vikki asked.

Google told me they were in the West Indies in January and February for a two-Test series followed by one-day internationals.

"Let's go," she said.

And so we booked: Antigua for the second Test. V needed something to look forward to and travel had always been her greatest incentive throughout the decade and more of her cancer. I had never enjoyed long-haul flights, and so we limited holidays together to Europe, but she loved the far-flung. Once a year, just before Christmas, she would take off for 10 days to Peru, Myanmar or Bhutan or some such exotic location. This time, I was willing to go with her. I was now aware that we were in the phase of "lasts". Many people use the phrase "bucket list" simply to mean a wish list. I was only too aware that it came from the phrase "kicking the bucket" and was about doing things before you died.

This forthcoming holiday period, we both unspokenly knew, would be V's last Christmas, for example. It was why we booked business class on British Airways and a suite at the best hotel on Antigua. Money hardly mattered any more. When first diagnosed, she had cashed in a critical-illness policy and had been saving as much of it as she could in case she needed expensive drugs or treatment in America. There was no need to save any more. It was for spending.

We also booked a pricy, beautiful hotel in Devon and went to see her friend Janet, a colleague years ago on the *Daily Mail* and maid of honour at our wedding, who now lived there. Though needing a stick, Vikki insisted on walking around Tavistock in a deluge.

And, after a Christmas Day at home alone, with my daughter Alex now living in Singapore, son Jack spending the time with his mother's – my first wife's – family, and V's mum Jean in a care home with vascular dementia, we headed early in the new year for one of our favourite places, Southwold in Suffolk, where V had bought for me a plaque on the pier dedicated to "my seaside boy". The trip would prove an ordeal rather than respite, however.

The hotel, newly modernised, was beautiful and the room ideal, overlooking the square. The view gave her some comfort as she could watch the coming and goings, the Christmas lights still illuminated. She did manage a meal out, or part of one, on the first night, a walk around the shops for half an hour on the second, and a stroll heavily reliant on her walking stick to the end of the pier on the third morning, but it was painful to watch and support. She was frustrated with herself, and that frustration – too much to bear alone – was also directed at me. So be it.

She had spurned the lightweight foldable wheel-chair we had bought. She wasn't ready for that just yet. Except that she was, not that I could suggest it. We drove to The Maltings at Snape, and took an hour to walk through the shops, she several times needing to sit down. Her stomach was now so bloated, her move-ment so limited, that I felt compelled to ring the Royal Marsden. She needed care, I told them. They agreed to find a bed for her.

Relief overwhelmed me. I was barely coping. Vikki was never one to feel sorry for herself, and her lack of self-pity made me ashamed to think that I would surely not be this resigned when my time came. Yet she was undoubtedly, and quite understandably, angry that it had come to this and fearful about what was to come next.

Twenty-four hours later, I was helping her settle back in to the Marsden, where over the next eight days she would have 10 litres of fluid drained from her stomach. This was simply to ease her distress. It was no cure, as meetings with palliative care teams confirmed. There would be arrangements for nurses from the local hospice, a hospital bed for the downstairs living room. V was still having none of it. She just wasn't that bad yet, she insisted. She may have known she was dying but she was not going gently into the long goodnight.

As a recovering alcoholic, I understood denial. I'd had it myself about my drinking in the 1980s, and seen enough of it down the years. I had come to understand enough about the illness to realise that denial existed to cut you off from the feelings of terror about your situation until the mind was ready to face reality and you were strong, or beaten, enough to take action.

(And despite her worsening state, Vikki had insisted on taking me for lunch that November to The Dorchester on the 30th anniversary of me quitting drinking. She knew the story of Grace O, the American woman whom AA's New York head office sent over to England in 1947 to help establish the fellowship in this country and who stayed at the hotel. Touchingly V wanted to mark the occasion there.)

As she sensed time closing in on her, she decided she wanted a meeting with the vicar, Rev. John, who had married us in our village. He was now semi-retired, looking after five parishes in Sussex. The day Vikki was discharged from the Marsden, after an eight-day stay this time, she insisted I drive her down and she spent an hour with him, discussing her funeral and her views on religion, while I sat in another room. She had found comfort, and company, in our local church, become a keen supporter and even attender, but always had reservations about an afterlife. Or as the priest who had succeeded John in our parish, Rev. Tom Sander, described it: "The terrifying issue of trust."

"John told me to look on it as another adventure. Like going to another country," V told me when we got back into the car. "I can live with that." She smiled after she said that last sentence. The irony of it was not lost on either of us.

Vikki also wanted me to find a solicitor for her to sort out her will and, as the time-worn phrase had it, to put her affairs in order. Things were moving apace. If she still wasn't ready to be treated physically as an invalid, she was now preparing mentally.

Then, a week after leaving hospital, she agreed to use the wheelchair. Actually I insisted, if we were going to be able to attend a dinner being held by the Football Writers' Association, of which she was vice-chair and had hoped to become the first female chair. It was a tribute night for the England manager Gareth Southgate at the Savoy Hotel in London and she was determined to get there. I'm sure she sensed, as did I, that this would be her last chance to connect with colleagues and the world in which she worked.

Over the next fortnight came last chances to connect with friends. Two close ones from university in Leicester, housemates at that time in the early 1980s, came to visit on successive Saturdays. One had told the other privately that it really was time to go and see her if she wanted to see her alive one more time. My daughter Alex also left her fiancé and job in Singapore for a week to spend some final time with her stepmother and offer me some welcome help.

Vikki was weakening by the day, the hour, and finally ended my fears about us going to Antigua. I was concerned about getting her through airports, a long flight – if the airline even allowed her to fly, that was – and about caring for her once there. She was barely eating now and would surely not have been able to make it to the cricket, even with a wheelchair. Just getting her in one to move from a room to a pool to relax and read would have been a trial.

Above all, I was petrified of her dying in my care and company, alone, halfway across the world and me having to repatriate her. I just did not want that burden, to be left alone in my pain with too many responsibilities to handle. Not that I could have said any of this to her. She would have been angry. The trick with Vikki – with all of us, I guess – was to let her reach her own conclusions.

After she did and I cancelled – with an understanding British Airways and hotel thankfully reimbursing us – I booked us a couple of days at a spa in the New Forest for the following week. I pretty much knew that we wouldn't make it but I wanted her again to have just a glimpse of something to look forward to.

When the first day of the Test began in Antigua, and I turned on the TV, she snapped at me to turn it off. It was insensitive of me, knowing that this was what we were missing. After all, while I may have the chance to go again, she knew she never would. It was similar to watching the news about Brexit. "Well, I'm not going to see it, whether it happens or not, am I?" she said, an edge in her voice when I made a comment about a news item. "So there's no point talking about it." It prompted a chilled, guilty silence in me.

On the second day of the Test, she told me to turn the TV on and smiled. The lure of the sunshine in the corner of the room had finally attracted her. Mind you, after a couple of days of watching England, I was ready to stop as well, so readily were they capitulating. We went back to watching *Four in a Bed* and *Say Yes to the Dress* as the mindless trash TV that was comforting her and occupying me. I wanted to be in the same room as her all the time by now, doing whatever she wanted to do. I had hoped for those six months the doctor had mentioned, but now I could see that was over-optimistic.

By the Friday, her temperature was spiking again at near 40 and she was dangerously weak. I called the Macmillan Nurse at the Marsden and the local hospice nurse on duty. I was told to ring 111 and ask for a duty GP to call.

When he eventually arrived, he performed a series of tests and went through some tick-box questions, concluding that some level or other was dangerously high. He insisted that Vikki needed to go to A&E for intravenous fluids. She baulked, as did I, but when a doctor from the Royal Marsden phoned to say she agreed with the recommendation, V – and I – finally listened.

Fearing the worst on a Friday night, I drove her over to one locally, though not the one of September that she

was now refusing to go back to. It was 8 p.m., ahead of
the pubs-closing rush, and thankfully she was hurried
through reception. What we were given to understand
would be a two-hour process, however, turned into one
of the worst nights of her, and my, life. And that was
saying something, given what we had been through over
the past year.

From reception to triage to A&E to ward... From vein
to vein in search of a spot for a cannula... It emerged that
they could not access her port – a device she had had sur-
gically inserted just under the skin in her chest six months
earlier at the Marsden, which could be used to inject
fluids – because nobody was qualified to do so. Finally,
they managed to gain some access in an emaciated arm
for the infusion drip that would raise her potassium level.

All against a backdrop of a department filling up with
emergency cases, most of them the worse for the effects
of alcohol and drugs. A young man was distressingly
wheeled into the cubicle opposite Vikki's, screaming and
struggling. The medics pinned him down while his father
sought to utter calming words in his ears as a combina-
tion of tranquilisers and time eased his heroin overdose.

By 2 a.m., he was sleeping and now V could relax a
little. She told me to go home to get some sleep as they
were keeping her in to see if they could get vitamins and
nourishing fluids into her. I had my misgivings but knew
I would be no use to her if I was too tired to act in her
best interests later in the day. When I returned half a

dozen hours later, they had not been able to pump anything into her and she was visibly upset. She wanted to
go home. I wanted her home. And so I took her home, via
wheelchair and car, wrapped in coat, scarf and blanket
against the winter chill.

She was grateful for the sanctuary, the warmth and
the familiarity of the house she had chosen for us in
Hertfordshire and into which we moved when I got back
from covering Euro 2004 in Portugal for *The Observer*.
(I felt sorry for the estate agent who told Vikki that he
needed to speak to me personally rather than simply take
her word that I had agreed to the purchase.) She rested
on the sofa. That second friend came from Paris to see
her, alerted by the first after the previous Saturday's visit
that now was the time.

Come bedtime, it took 15 minutes to manoeuvre,
support, cajole and frankly push her up the stairs. But it
was hard to push her, as by now she had no backside. It
had withered to skin. There was little to grasp without
hurting her.

"This is the last time," she said, finally and reluctantly surrendering. "It's time to get that hospital bed."

My anxiety about her raised temperature, erratic
breathing and restlessness stopped me sleeping for more
than an odd hour, and by morning, while not quite at
my wit's end, I could see its approaching headlights. I
rang the hospice. I needed help, I said. I just couldn't
cope any more.

Though it was a Sunday, a nurse arrived, an assistant soon after, and thankfully took charge. She asked me to bring a single bed down for Vikki and, with the help of a friend from the village, we assembled it and settled V in it. It would have to suffice for a day or two until they could get a hospital bed with a foot pedal for tilting her up and down, which she liked. Vikki, now in and out of sleep and with liquid morphine coursing through her, called it a "pumpy bed".

I was in awe of the nurse's tricks of the trade, from giving her water through a syringe – she was now struggling to drink it even through a straw – to getting me to cut up melon into small cubes and freeze it so that Vikki could have it cool and feel it melt on her tongue. I was hugely relieved. I no longer felt so alone and so helpless.

When night fell, I brought down a mattress to sleep on the floor alongside her. There would again be little sleep, though. Come 2 a.m., her voice penetrated the lightness of my doze to the point where I couldn't be sure if I was dreaming or it was really Vikki.

"Music. I want music," she said. "Nice things."

I rushed from my mattress to the CD player and combed the shelves for something she might like.

"Why haven't you done this already?" she demanded, growing agitated. Because, I did not say, I thought we had longer than this.

My 60th birthday weekend four years earlier sprang to my mind. I had asked everybody to choose their "inheritance" tracks, a feature from BBC Radio 4's *Saturday Live* show. My guests at a rented house in the Cotswolds had to choose one piece of music they had inherited and one they would pass on. Vikki had chosen a passage from the jazz pianist Keith Jarrett's seminal Cologne concert to pass on.

She, almost blokishly, had stacked her CDs alphabetically and I found Keith Jarrett easily enough. She loved his playing. In the half-light of a candle, though, I couldn't find the Cologne concert. Instead, I found one I couldn't remember having played before. It was called *The Melody At Night, With You.* The title appealed and I hastily stuffed it into the CD player.

Some years before, V had taken me to the Antibes Jazz Festival to see him. We stayed just across the road at a little hotel she had found. She was so brilliant at finding great hotels and restaurants. I didn't really appreciate the music of Keith Jarrett. For me, raised on rock and pop as a teenager in the 1970s, the word jazz always made me recoil. But I went to Antibes for V, whose cancer had not long returned at that time, and anyway, it was a holiday in the South of France. How bad could that be? I was happy she was happy and that she enjoyed the music. Me? I could always look out on the Mediterranean.

On this night now, from the first notes of his virtuoso piano-playing on the opening track "I Loves You Porgy" from Porgy and Bess, she relaxed and consequently so did I. The whole album was unspeakably, tearfully beautiful. I lay awake and listened to all 55 minutes, spellbound, grateful that Vikki was soothed.

The next morning, Vikki asked for two friends from the village, a retired judge and an ex-solicitor, to call in to witness her will. Local friends also came, Moira bringing snowdrops from her garden to put on V's bedside table. By late afternoon, she was becoming disorientated, calling for the hospital bed. It was on its way, I told her, and would definitely be here in the morning. By the middle of the night, she was again agitated and this time calling for a news channel on the TV. Once more there would be little sleep, though Keith Jarrett helped again. Who could blame her if the darkness and the loneliness terrified her? She needed voices.

By the time two representatives of her employers at *The Sun* came to see her the next morning for a meeting she had brought forward, her conversation had grown limited and they would not stay long. She called for the "pumpy" bed again and thankfully it arrived. More able to get into a comfortable position in an adjustable bed, she relaxed.

As did I when the hospice people told me they could get a Marie Curie nurse to oversee V tonight so that I would be able to go upstairs to bed and get a night's sleep. I accepted gratefully. Vicar Tom was also coming. He had offered to say prayers for her at her bedside and I agreed, though any last rites felt premature. I told him that she might have several days yet but he said that it was no bother; he could come again. These were just prayers to nurture her and me. His presence, his words, when he came around 8 p.m., were comforting to me at least. His main audience was by now in no condition to take in much as her sleep was deep.

By the time Bibi the Marie Curie nurse arrived at 10 p.m., bringing with her all that remained good about people in the service of others, I was ready for some rest. V had been in and out of sleep for several hours, just taking water and morphine orally through a syringe. A nurse would be coming the next day to fit a morphine pump into a vein as she was now having trouble swallowing anything.

I grabbed my chance to get some sleep. It was never going to be deep, given my concerns about Vikki downstairs, but I drifted off to the sounds of the midnight news on Radio 4.

Just over four hours later, I was startled by a knock at the bedroom door. Bibi suggested I should come downstairs as Vikki's breathing had changed. I dashed down and clutched her hand. She lay on her back, her eyes closed. Her breathing was indeed short and shallow. Soon it would be non-existent.

· 4 ·

"Would You Like to Brush Her Hair?"

Vikki Michelle Orvice died at precisely 5.02 a.m. on Wednesday 6 February 2019. Or, more precisely, at 5.12 a.m. Bibi said we needed to wait 10 minutes without her breathing for it to be certain that she was dead.

I had seen a beloved uncle die and heard then what I had only read about before: a death rattle. For several hours, a series of intermittent sounds emerged from his throat, sounding similar to snoring but more ominous and threatening. I had also watched my unconscious father die a slow death over eight days, hallucinating at times. I had feared one or the other, or indeed both, for Vikki.

Instead, she slipped away peacefully and even swiftly. I now understood why people used the word slipped, and indeed the phrase "passed away". Some decry the words as euphemisms – for the brutal pedants, of course I knew she had died, was dead, and nothing could make that better – but they seem to describe what happened with Vikki. She slipped away. She passed.

Bibi said that V had woken momentarily in the night to request morphine, and a small dose had been administered, and I was jealous of the nurse that V had communicated with her when I was not there. All I could do now was light candles and tea lights and put Keith Jarrett in the CD player.

And talk to her and tell her I loved her and that I would miss her so much.

(I didn't know how much just then.)

I kissed her forehead.

(And I weep as I write that sentence and feel the need to do something, anything – checking my Twitter feed, email and Facebook – before writing the next one, yet I know I need to feel, to endure, this sadness and pain rather than avoid it.)

She couldn't speak back, of course, but the perceived wisdom is that the dying can hear all you say. I wondered what my last words to her had been when she was semi-conscious yesterday. I found I couldn't remember. And so I hoped it was true that she could indeed hear my love for her.

Though my breaking heart pounded, in contrast to hers now stilled, only when Bibi confirmed that she was indeed dead did I weep. There was no longer the panic of that November day three months ago, nor my gasping inarticulacy as I saw her, eyes rolling, on the floor of the CAU at the Marsden. This was more a say-it-ain't-so sadness. A realisation that the fateful time had come, three months sooner than I had expected.

Was it here now that the grief that had been dormant would manifest itself? I was a widower. (How I would come to hate that word. I felt sure I would forever describe myself instead as Vikki's husband.) I had a late wife. I still didn't know about the grief I feared, couldn't tell you if it had arrived. I thought that with the first shafts of the light of morning would come mourning. Instead, it was numbness.

I lose track here of who came to the house first, but I remember Bibi making a phone call and two nurses arriving around 6 a.m. Was one a district nurse, one from the hospice organisation? I do recall Bibi taking her leave with the first of thousands of condolences that would arrive and take me by surprise in the coming hours. I also remember giving her as thanks a copy of a book I had ghostwritten, *Sober* by Tony Adams. The night before we had talked about football. She was a Liverpool fan, she said.

The two nurses, meanwhile, though sympathetic and supportive, necessarily busied themselves with the tasks of death with which they were familiar. Even if I wasn't. While one attended to the paperwork that would tell of time and cause of death for Vikki's GP later to issue more paperwork, the other tended to Vikki, making her look comfortable.

"She's smiling," she said and it was true that Vikki did have a look of serenity, almost satisfaction on her face. I'm not sure if it was said to comfort and console me. Whatever, it did and I was grateful.

Then came a question I would be forever thankful for the chance to answer and which gave me the most precious, intimate and tender moment of my life.

"Would you like to brush her hair?" the nurse asked and I accepted eagerly the invitation.

(And again, as I write, the urge descends to check email, Twitter and Facebook as diversion from the bitter-sweetness of the memory.)

Vikki's hair these days, such as it was after years of battering by chemotherapy, was short and thick and grey, unlike the immaculately styled, sleek raven-hued chevelure that I had known when I first met her 23 years earlier. It really didn't need much brushing. But I stroked and cajoled the soft bristles through it until I might have begun to look a little too obsessive to the nurses.

By 7 a.m. their work was finished and they said that at some point, today if possible, I should pick up a document from our GP practice and then take it to the local registry office so that I could obtain a death certificate, which would be needed before I could organise a funeral.

They asked if I had an undertaker in mind. I didn't but Vikki did. In preparing for her death and her funeral, she had left comprehensive instructions during the previous week. Indeed, she had emailed me two A4 pages' worth. A friend in the village had given her the name of the most efficient and best-value funeral directors in the area.

I couldn't bring myself to ring them for now. It would be something final, would mean that they would have to come and take her body away. I wanted just to sit here, in peace and solitude, curtains closed, and be with her for a while longer. Down the years, I had read of people who keep their dead partner's body in the house for days and weeks. It had always struck me as ghoulish, weird. This morning, I had a glimmer of understanding how they felt.

It was now around 7.30 a.m. and I decided I should text what little family she had left – cousins, mainly – to give them the bad news. Vikki's father, Fred, had died in 1996 and it would have been cruel to inform her 88-year-old dementia-stricken mother, Jean. Then her stepchildren and my family. After that, close friends, particularly in the village, and the sports editor of her newspaper so that he could inform all her colleagues.

And the vicar. He now came to perform prayers of commendation, asking that God accept her. The light was filtering through but I kept the curtains drawn.

By around 8.15 a.m., it was just me and her. In her more lucid moments of the previous weekend, she had asked that I should announce her death on Facebook and Twitter (me saying "Please, Vikki, let's not talk about it yet") as there would simply be too many people in her professional life to inform individually. At 9 a.m., sitting in an armchair at her bedside, I dutifully did as she'd requested and it read:

My beloved, bright, brilliant wife Vikki Orvice passed away at 5am, able to defy the cancer no longer. I am bereft, empty, but grateful for her life and her love. Those who feel the breath of sadness, sit down next to me.

The last sentence was a quotation from the song "Sit Down" by James, a Manchester band of the 1990s we both loved and had seen in concert at the Royal Albert Hall together, Vikki dancing typically enthusiastically once she got going. It just came into my mind as I typed.

What happened next was astonishing.

Replies rained in torrentially from family and close friends, acquaintances and strangers, the celebrated in the world of media and sport. Those such as her fellow Sheffielder Lord Sebastian Coe, footballers Gary Neville and Tony Adams, athletes Jessica Ennis-Hill, Kelly Holmes, Paula Radcliffe and Adam Gemili offered me their sympathy, and Vikki their sadness. Sporting governing bodies and football clubs joined in.

I sat at her bedside and watched them all arrive on my phone, spellbound. There were text messages and phone calls too but I could not bring myself to answer them. "Look at this, Vikki," I said. "I wish you could see this." Talking to her would become commonplace and I could not resist noting the irony of her not interrupting me. I would come to lament that silence, though; would give anything to be interrupted.

Some messages and tweets I felt needed a response, including the sympathy of Tim Booth, the singer of James, whose song I had quoted. And I wanted to thank the local hospice, the Royal Marsden Hospital and the nurse Bibi for ensuring that I was awake, and present, senses heightened, when Vikki died. Mostly for now, though, I could only thank people generally. There were simply too many to reply to individually.

At one point, Vikki was even trending on Twitter. She would have found it amusing. Actually, I think she would have loved it. In fact, the following day I would tweet:

The saddest bit today is wanting to show her, to say: "Look, Vikki. This is what you meant to everyone" but she can't see or hear. I think and hope she knew. From me for sure. Anyway, tell someone today what they mean to you while you can.

By nature, journalists are competitive. They are looking to scoop their rivals, to show their boss and their paper that they are alert and good at what they do. It can lead to wanting to do others down before they do you down. And while colleagues become friends, through shared hardships and overseas assignments, all are aware that the profession can be a battleground. It was especially acute for Vikki as a woman in what had for too long been a man's world and she often had to fight to get her stories printed and used properly.

Given the dynamics of Fleet Street, and public attitudes towards journalists these days, it was the generosity of spirit, I think, that would have surprised her most amid this outpouring of admiration and affection for her. I knew she was well respected, and particularly popular in athletics having covered the sport for 20 years, but this was something else.

She had just got on with the job, but her achievement of being the first female football writer appointed to the staff of a national tabloid newspaper, back in 1995, had clearly reverberated far and wide, long and loud.

By 2 p.m., nine hours after her death and six of sitting alone with her, I began to feel that I really ought now to ring the funeral directors. By 3 p.m. they had arrived. A kindly middle-aged man knocked on the door, his deferential, respectful manner honed by years of comforting experience.

He told me that it might be as well if I adjourned to another room while he and his colleague transferred the body from the bed to their vehicle. I hadn't seen what they'd arrived in – hearse, van? – as I had no wish to open the curtains but I did know what they meant. She was leaving in a body bag.

Then she was gone. Then the house was empty.

* * *

I look back on the time immediately after the undertakers took Vikki's body and I recall a cacophony of thoughts and feelings competing frenziedly for attention. Over-whelmingly, I felt pity. Pity for poor V. She was only 56 years old. It was – as many people would venture in the phrase designed to convey their sadness and sympathy – no age. I could weep for her. I did weep for her.

I have to admit, too, to feeling some relief in the imme-diate aftermath of her death. Yes, at first it was a little to do with no longer having all my waking hours – at least 20 a day – preoccupied with caring for her, with fetching and carrying, washing and wiping. But then, I soon realised, I had actually come to enjoy those tasks. As a young man, my squeamishness and selfishness would have been unable to contemplate any of the privations of the last year, but as her husband who loved her deeply, I came to see those acts as moments of shared intimacy. As privileges.

No, my relief was more that the sheer worry was over. The worry about her daily ups and downs, emo-tionally and physically. I was also relieved for her, that she would no longer be in the pain that was requiring more and more morphine, that she would no more be in and out of hospitals where they would search for veins from which to take out blood or to pump in nourish-ment. Relieved that her stomach would no longer bloat nor her limbs waste.

So there, in two heartbeats, was already the dou-ble-edged sword of grief. I was relieved that it was over, for both of us. I was desperately sad that it was over. For both of us.

Now what? What next? What was the procedure? As I sat in an empty house, trying to process conflicting emotions, it occurred that I should do what I always did. Make a to-do list. As if one cannot take too much, too soon, of the grief, I felt called into action. I can't remember crying over a to-do list before, mind.

The house may have been empty of people but it was still cluttered with the paraphernalia of illness. In the lounge, the sofas had been pushed to the walls, my armchair to the bedside for visitors, but it was still an obstacle course. As well as the hospital bed, there was a commode, a new reclining chair that Vikki had ordered but never got to use, and the other single bed I had brought down and on which I was planning to sleep once I'd had that night off in our own bed upstairs.

Now there were jobs to be done. The chores of bereavement – what I've heard called "sadmin". I had to go to the doctor to pick up the form that listed a cause of death. It was a requirement before a death certificate could be issued. I then had to arrange an appointment to get that death certificate at the local registry office.

And I wanted all this hospital equipment – bed, commode, stool for the bath upstairs (unused) – out of the house. I rang the company that had supplied it all. It would be a week before they could get anyone to me, they said.

"No, it won't," I replied. "Today, I have lost my wife and I no longer want those things in my house. You will come tomorrow, please."

They would come tomorrow, they said.

Sometimes you read about couples who never spent nights apart. Given our work as sports journalists, we had spent plenty alone. And to be honest, as I'm sure Vikki felt too, it was on occasion good to have some room to spread out and not have to worry about lights-out time when the other was ready to sleep and sighing loudly to make a point.

So having the double bed to myself tonight, made little difference for now. I was used to it. Nothing much had yet hit me. I did a crossword. Listened to the midnight news on Radio 4, after which I usually fell asleep. Here was something new, however. I was still awake for the soothing strains of "Sailing By" and the *Shipping Forecast*. And then the start of the World Service. And every couple of hours thereafter due to the curse of the prostate. And the need to cry.

I just had to be awake – and thankfully was, after a couple of hours of fitful dozing – for the sports bulletin of the *Today* programme. The phone line was bad but I could just make out an appreciation of Vikki by her colleague and the co-founder of the organisation for whom V was a board member, Women in Football, Anna Kessel. Anna would later tell me that the producers were trying to get the presenter Karthi Gnanasegaram to wrap it up due to the crackly line but she and Anna were determined to plough on.

That presaged four pages of obituary and tributes in *The Sun*. They even wrote a leader about "Our Vikki". I had phoned the head of sport, Shaun Custis, her boss, a few days before to prime him, and to ask that Steve Howard, now retired as chief sports writer but whom Vikki respected greatly and who had been on overseas assignments with her, should write it. It was, naturally, magnificent.

That morning there were more chores. More on the to-do list. Through moist eyes, I stripped the loaned hospital bed, ready for the company to collect it. I removed the bedding and threw it away. Because bodies relax at their death, and functions go uncontrolled, the sheets were soiled. So too the plastic mattress. I wiped the urine and excrement from it. I was happy, even grateful, to do so. It was the last part of Vikki. I wanted to remain close to her and this was one way of doing it.

I was just about ready to take the odd call from family, mainly Vikki's, and our closest friends. Otherwise I let my mobile ring and buzz with texts, watched my email inbox fill up. I checked Twitter and Facebook. It continued to be overwhelming. The numbers were clicking like a football turnstile. Eventually, staggeringly, there would be more than 1,500 replies, some 750 retweets and almost 21,000 likes of my original tweet.

Gradually I began to get our living room back. Make that *my* living room. Would I ever get used to swapping the one possessive pronoun for the other? Still, though, the recliner sat there, ugly but practical, and would do for another few days yet, as if waiting for Thora Hird to come and sit in it rather than the understanding York-shire company to collect it.

By now, I was in something of a daze and I felt I needed space and solitude. I went to sit in our local church for half an hour before going to see the vicar to discuss the funeral. Vikki and I had such history in St Leonard's with its quaint, pointed Hertfordshire steeple. It was another way of reconnecting with her.

I went to the vicarage armed with two sheets of paper I had printed out. Her instructions for the funeral, emailed to me four days before she died, said so much about her, about her pragmatism and the fastidiousness that made her such a good journalist.

Subject: funeral logistics

Weston's Funeral directors – Harpenden.
Plot – god's acre.

No flowers – retiring collection for Royal Marsden.
Bunch of long-stemmed cream roses from family on top of coffin (jackie Scopes will do this) NO sunflowers!

Dress – Black or Bright

Coffin to be brought to church day before and kept overnight so in place.

Welcome address by canon John green.

Hymn
Guide Me O Thou Great Redeemer (gospel choir to

lead if they can although not on set list. If not rousing
enough)

Reading
Psalm 121
Read by Janet King

HYMN
Thine Be the Glory

Letter from Vikki to be read by Ian Ridley plus eulogy
from Ian Ridley.

Gospel choir – O Happy Day
Say a Little Prayer
Something Inside so Strong

Reading
          by Julia Darling
Read by Claire Smith

Prayers
The Lord's Prayer

HYMN
Jerusalem

During the exit of the coffin
The Way You Look Tonight by Jerome Kern
Played by Alexandra Ridley

Coffin to be taken to God's Acre for burial.
Congregation welcome to join family for burial OR walk
over to village hall where food, tea and coffee (and one
glass of wine each are)

Programme – A celebration of the Life of Vikki Orvice 1962– on front. I want it PLAIN. No pic on front. On back picture of me in Sydney. Underneath wording "Life Taught Me to Die".

Village hall has to be booked separately through Phil Oswin or Jane Iutman – numbers in parish magazine – but if we have at least a three week run-in and given we avoid Saturdays for obvious reasons it should be ok. Given they only have those small tables with paper tablecloths get Jasper's in who we used at wedding for proper round tables and tablecloths etc. Prob ok with chairs but depending on numbers they can do those too. Moira will help with food ie M&S or the company we used for the wedding do buffet quotes once you have numbers. Wine from Aldi. I can transfer money from my current account to Co-Op account to cover all costs.

You will have to contact Grapevine as well – letting village know so they can devour big baps and also warning them re parking (Mark will no doubt help with parking if needed!) if numbers do rise. I know they did this with the young mum who died late last year of cancer in the village.

Re wording on grave-stone (I think the funeral directors sort out stone if needed) keep it simple ie Vikki Orvice 1962–

Similarly keep the coffin simple. Nothing heavy, oak or fancy. And no wickerwork or hamper baskets (they work out pricier anyway I'm told!).

For those tempted to point out the errors of spelling and punctuation, bear in mind that this is the work of a woman less than a week away from her death. God's Acre, by the way, is the pretty little cemetery on the hill in the village, about 100 yards from the church, where she would be buried. Grapevine was an email network of people in the village.

And big baps? A joke between us. Whenever we went to a Northern funeral, it always seemed that the wake featured thick cob rolls, cut in half and stuffed with wedges of cheese or doorsteps of ham. We would laugh about it on the drive up and then eye each other and smile when we turned up, usually in the back room of a pub, to see the generous "baps" laid out.

As the day wore on, and messages and media coverage piled up, it was clear that getting sandwiches from M&S and wine from Aldi was not going to get the job done. An email sending condolences from the Football Writers' Association said that one of the members had remarked: "I hope it's a bloody big church."

It wasn't. It seated about 120, with room for about that number standing. Over the next few days I soon began to fret about how to organise this. It didn't help that I was walking around in slow motion, partly through lack of sleep. I was only half-finishing tasks; leaving a bin bag on the doorstep rather than depositing it in a bin. I found myself in front of the bathroom mirror staring at my weeping face with a pint of milk in my hand.

As for other domestic tasks, I had little stomach for them. The little washing bowl – or rather a Tupperware container the nurse had located – that we had kept at Vikki's bedside was going to stay by the sink for now, along with the soft children's toothbrush that I had bought her so we could brush her teeth more gently.

I recall my reverie as I gazed at it one mid-morning being interrupted by the thump of some post arriving through the letterbox. It contained, somewhat belatedly, an athletics calendar for the year ahead, addressed to Vikki. Meanwhile upstairs on her desk, she had cut out an article on "10 Young Athletes to Watch in 2019" from a magazine.

It was hard to know what was grief – if I even recognised it yet – or just shock. I felt numb, for sure, and sad. But the magnitude of what had happened had still not fully registered, what with worrying about this funeral. Besides, being distracted and having a short attention span could be attributed to the ageing process.

Shopping, when I could make it out of the house, was an assault course. I would pick up two steaks out of habit. And after 15 minutes in a supermarket, I would become overwhelmed by the volume of people and the wealth of choice. Indecision gnawed at me. On one occasion, I simply fled, putting the half-filled basket down in an aisle. After that, I wrote short lists of the essentials and tried to be in and out in about 10 minutes.

I do recall passing a clothes shop where, a few weeks before she died, I had taken Vikki to buy some trousers that might fit her now-smaller waist and thinner legs. She had struck up a conversation with the young sales assistant whose mother was undergoing chemotherapy. Today, I felt compelled to go in and tell her of Vikki's death, to urge her to enjoy her mother for as long as she was alive. She remembered Vikki. Everyone did. As our friend Moira had told me a friend had said to her of V: "Once met, never forgotten." I felt bad afterwards, that perhaps I shouldn't have shared V's passing with the girl in the shop, though she had thanked me for my sentiments.

When it came to cooking, if I did feel hungry and could be bothered to cook, I just couldn't work out how many peas were enough for one. Indeed, food was getting wasted as I bought and cooked too much. Two steaks, two pieces of salmon. It didn't occur to me, in my fuddled state, that I could freeze the other one. How V hated waste. Another reason for me to feel guilty. For now, I would go back to ready meals. I had done most of the cooking during the worsening of her illness these past 16 months. Giving the microwave some use couldn't hurt just for a while.

After several days of this, I knew I had to snap out of it. For Vikki's sake. The tributes to her were piling up, as were requests for funeral information. I needed to get to work if she was to have the send-off she deserved.

As Robert Shaw said in *Jaws*, we were going to need a bigger boat.

· 5 ·

Rites of Passage and Passing

The logistics of death can be distracting, diverting and even welcome. I guess they form part of the denial that is talked about – that she is gone for good (strange expression, now I think about it; there is nothing good), that she is not coming back. It was just too much to absorb in those early days. As with my and other addicts' experience, denial can keep you in the pain but it can also become almost protectively familiar. I was happy – no, make that less unhappy – in its embrace just now. And the logistics of death can occupy the seconds, minutes and hours of what makes up the time that people say is the healer.

By now, Vikki was almost a public figure. I didn't expect – and I'm certain that she wouldn't have – the volume of respect for her from athletes, footballers, sports administrators and journalists. On the day of her death, articles quickly sprang up online. Soon full obituaries would appear. *The Times* rang me for anecdotes for theirs and I was happy to supply them. Another obit appeared in the *Daily Telegraph*, while *The Last Word* on Radio 4 accorded her several minutes of air time.

Vikki would have so loved that the life of a working-class lass from south Sheffield was being marked in the newspaper of record, as well as the house journal of the Conservative Party (given our left-of-centre politics), and that her favourite radio station was marking her life and death.

Shortly after Vikki's death, I was also invited by Liz Birchall, UK Athletics' head of communications, who had become friends with V, to the British indoor athletics trials in Birmingham. I went with another Liz, Vikki's best friend at school in Sheffield. The stadium announcer, Katharine Merry, read her touching obituary before a minute's applause. It was a remarkable moment.

(Kath, by the way, Olympic 400 metres bronze medallist in 2000, had also become friends with Vikki. I recall V that night ringing me from inside the stadium in Sydney. It was her first major night in the job of athletics correspondent and she was nervous. I told her that big players rose to big occasions. And she did.)

I found myself now wishing that Vikki had realised more how loved and respected she was during her life, that she might have seen journalism less often as the battleground that could be so draining. Her friend Jayne Pearce-McMenamin, in charge of media arrangements for so many major events including London 2012, contacted me to say she was naming the press room at the European Indoor Athletics Championships in Glasgow after Vikki. The London Marathon would do the same in April, and in May I would be invited to the Women's FA Cup final at Wembley in V's honour. They wrote an article in the match-day programme.

To many, she appeared tough, willing and able to fight her corner, to stand for no nonsense. And she was and did. I saw the price she paid sometimes for it, however. I saw her come home in tears from an event where she had argued with another journalist who had accused her of stealing quotes from a famous athlete (as if Vikki ever needed to; her contacts filled a Filofax). I would hear her arguing with a news editor on the phone then put it down and begin crying at the frustration and fear of losing her job.

I also recalled the incidents and episodes she had endured while covering football and which she handled with humour and aplomb but that had made her defensive at times; of football managers who looked at her while making laddish, lewd remarks, trying to embarrass her. There was one who swore copiously in front of her then told the other – male – reporters not to worry as she liked it when men talked dirty to her. There was another who made a remark about the astonishing size of his goalkeeper's penis, making eye contact with Vikki all the while. She, calling his bluff, asked if she could have the custodian's phone number. There was also the manager who asked her out, seeking to profit from his position of power.

As an example of what she had to put up with – and she also told me of things other women endured, like the reporter interviewing a manager who began stroking her hair – she found out during her early days at *The Sun* that one colleague had said to another they "would have her out of here in tears in a week." It was little known that she did in fact go back to her old news editor at the *Daily Mail*, where she'd been consumer affairs correspondent, to enquire if her old job was still available. He told her not to give in, to stick at it.

(And while recalling the misogyny she faced, I found it ironic that a Sky Sports chat show for football writers on the Sunday following her death would note her passing and pay tribute. This was a programme that never invited her on despite her patent qualifications. I had been on it many times. My daughter called it "Four Fat Blokes Round A Table".)

Then there was the plain funny – the press room steward at a Premier League club who checked with her whether she thought they had made enough sandwiches for the reporters. And the head of the Cyprus FA who asked her, while she was covering an England Under-21 game there, why she was not at home, "making beautiful things".

Now she was being routinely referred to as a trailblazer and a pioneer who had packed so much into her career. My Vikki. My privately vulnerable and self-doubting Vikki, always determined to keep delivering, even with the cancer and the chemo and the side effects. I had regularly seen her file copy from a chemo chair at the Marsden while potent drugs were being pumped into her body.

I set to work on a funeral to do her proud, frozen at first by the size of the task but surrounded by sympathy. Vikki's friends in the village were especially caring and they would become my friends too. One lovely lady knocked on the door with a dish of pasta and bolognese. Another brought a lamb tagine for the freezer. Over the next few weeks, they would become my organising committee for an event that her boss at *The Sun* – the paper supportive to me and helping with finance and organisational help – would describe as "like a state funeral".

Cards from acquaintances, with heartfelt sentiments, dropped regularly through the letterbox but the figures who delivered them had often hurried away by the time I looked out of the window. Eye contact would be difficult, I guess. Via post came handwritten letters of sympathy. Rare, but welcome.

It was important that I didn't get ill with so much to be done and this was February, the season of colds and flus. I made special efforts to take care of myself, now eating regularly and sleeping as much as possible, though it would just be a few hours here and there. I simply could not afford to miss my own wife's funeral, particularly given that she had charged me with delivering a eulogy for her. I was determined to make it the best thing I had ever written.

The gospel choir was the first booking. Then there was an overspill marquee, and a company to film and relay the service into the marquee. There were professional caterers, car park and seating plans to organise. Fortunately, much of it was taken out of my hands. The village committee swung into action. *The Sun*'s sports desk secretary, Rachel Deegan, took on catering and marquee arrangements.

I assembled photo after photo of V, from my phone and hers (to which she had once given me the PIN code) and made trip after trip to Boots to print them off so that they could be fixed to large white art boards that I could hang in the marquee to tell the story of her remarkable, and remarkably full, life.

A week after Vikki's death, I asked to visit the chapel of rest where her open coffin lay, and the undertaker met me there with a key. I wondered how I would be, how she would look, and went with trepidation. But I so wanted to see her face one last time. She looked at peace, pain-free, and was now wearing the beautiful red rose-patterned outfit she had worn when representing a breast cancer charity at a Buckingham Palace garden party on a magical May day the previous year and in which I now wanted her buried. The chapel room was icy with February chill but I sat with her for as long as I could, talking to her. I kissed her forehead. I couldn't resist taking one last photo of her in her finery. A photo that only I would ever see.

On the day before her burial, the undertakers brought her to the church at sunset, in line with her request, and I sat with her now closed casket on my own, as I did at dawn on the day itself. I knew I would have to share her with so many on the day of the funeral. I needed to recall that she was my wife, a human being, strong yet frail, who could not be defined solely as a pioneering journalistic figure. She was my love, a daughter, a stepmother.

The day itself proved to be the warmest February day for decades, people wearing light suits and dresses, barely a cloud in the sky. No matter the cost, I was desperate for her to have a memorable send-off. The church bells rang, the gospel choir sang and almost 500 people turned up.

Among them, beyond family and friends, were figures such as Paula Radcliffe, Jessica Ennis-Hill, Dina Asher-Smith and Adam Gemili, Tony Adams and his fellow former Arsenal player Alan Smith, and world champion boxer Darren Barker. Governing bodies of athletics and football, along with the British Olympic Association, were represented. *The Sun* sent their top brass. We put their sports reporters in the choir stalls. V would have enjoyed that.

Her friends read the readings she requested, including the poignant poem by Julia Darling entitled "How to Behave around the Ill", and I relayed her final message, which had people laughing and crying by turn.

"I think *Private Eye*'s Street of Shame – a rite of passage in any journalist's career – once described me as 'feisty' and 'shirty'," she wrote. "Well, no excuses, but it was only because I cared. Thanks though to those who stuck with me along the way.

"I've had the most amazing life and being first diagnosed 12 years ago tends to focus your priorities, so I was able to pack in trips to weird and wonderful places both through work and on holidays."

Her beloved football team, Sheffield United – who were represented at the funeral by her favourite player, Tony Currie (we had a signed photo of him in our downstairs loo) – were not going to go unmentioned.

"Sheffield United, though, I fear are going to bottle it again," she wrote. "A whiff of automatic promotion and they crumble…" (A few months later, she would be wrong, for one of the very few times in her life.)

"On that note we don't want people to be sad today," she continued. "What happens now is another adventure, another country to visit, a test of trust and hope. So please try and remember the good things. And good things in your life too.

"As for that offside rule… I'm still working on it!"

Spontaneous applause, long and loud, broke out in the church.

How could my eulogy follow that with anything as remotely touching and witty? All I could do was justice, pausing midway through to ask the broadcaster and her fellow board member at Women in Football, Jacqui Oatley, to read a message from Lord Coe.

"She came into our lives for just a short time but her impact was profound," he noted. "She will be loved and remembered by so many, me amongst them, for a very long time."

I told of her life so well lived, her career – the highlight being London 2012 and Super Saturday – and of all the committees and organisations she served, including six years as a patient governor for the Royal Marsden. Of how at dinners she hated me introducing myself with: "Hello, I'm Denis Thatcher."

I even told my favourite story of the time when we were sitting next to Sir Bobby Robson at a Football Writers' Association dinner. "Vikki has cancer as well," I said to Bobby. "What type?" he asked her. "Well, they think the primary was breast but it could have been ovarian," she replied. "Them, pet," Bobby said, "are the only two I've not had."

She had asked that I be honest about her. "The tensions of cancer take their toll," my eulogy added. "We had our ups and downs, as those who knew us well would testify. But they came too with love, passion, a shared sense of humour and cultural interests. Anyway, ups and downs are the rhythm of life. Like the movements on a cardiograph, they show you're alive. And how alive Vikki was.

"She was gregarious, tender, vulnerable, warm-hearted and funny, with a smile as wide as the M1 at

Tinsley Viaduct. She was waspishly witty and I wasn't spared. When I came home from the British Press Awards with the Sports Journalist of the Year trophy 12 years ago, she was in bed and looked up from her book to say: 'I told you it was a Zara Phillips kind of year.'

"Yours was not a long life, but better one short and broad – of mind, achievement and adventure – rather than long and narrow. Goodnight, my Saturday girl."

Afterwards, we all processed down the village high street to the cemetery and I threw a white rose on her lowered coffin. Somebody pointed out that the whole event, though it was not planned that way, lasted an appropriate 90 minutes.

And then I tried to smile amid a haze of tea, sandwiches and faces.

My daughter Alex, my rock through this, stayed a few days more before having to get back to her job and fiancé in Singapore. Once she was gone, the house was empty. More than that, with Vikki now in the ground, my world was empty.

Alone, three weeks on now from Vikki's death, that Melanie song "Leftover Wine" went through my mind again. And I wondered what you do when all of the people go home.

· 6 ·

Wight and Shade

One Sunday in late May, I drove to Southsea, where I had booked a room in a Premier Inn ahead of taking the hovercraft to Ryde on the Isle of Wight on the Monday morning. From there I would take a taxi to the ground near Newport that was hosting the opening day of Hampshire v Nottinghamshire in Division One of the County Championship.

It was nine months since I had last stayed in this hotel, ahead of visiting my therapist Bruce, whose main home, away from his London office, was on the island. We could have longer sessions here. It had been summer, that hot summer of 2018. Vikki was alive then, ill but alive enough to go to the European Athletics Championships in Berlin. That horrendous September, when all the infections set in and she would spend 23 days in hospital, was a few weeks away yet.

From the window of the hotel back then I'd watched a knockabout 20-over club cricket match on an adjacent playing field. This time there was no such entertainment and the Sunday blues enveloped me. A walk along Southsea promenade barely helped, though it was a pleasant evening. Little was open save for amusement arcades. I knew from my previous visit that there was just an odorous fast food joint here (and the burger last time had been disgusting) so I called in to see old friends near Southampton who had offered me a welcome meal.

Tea and biscuits sustained me through the usual wakeful night until it was time to walk the few minutes to the hoverport. In the terminal, there looked to be just a few going to the cricket. I expected more, thought it would be a big attraction. I bought a coffee from the machine and sat, alternately gazing out on to the Solent and contemplating the dirty grey carpet.

The terminal's speakers were tuned to Magic FM. Barry White's "You're The First, My Last, My Everything" came on and I couldn't help smiling. It reminded me of a holiday with Vikki at a gorgeous hotel at Ravello on the Amalfi coast of Italy (she found it, of course), when big Barry's greatest hits would come on over breakfast – incongruously, given the well-heeled clientele – and I would sashay across the dining room to get my eggs with V laughing in the background. It had prompted me to buy the CD when we got back home so I could amuse her with some dad-dancing across the living room now and then.

The day was overcast and grey, the crossing short and smooth, unlike one I recalled years earlier when asked to go to Cowes Week for the *Daily Telegraph* and write a colour piece, only to arrive through high winds and stormy seas to find there had been two deaths, of crewmen being swept overboard.

Once on the island this time, the taxi driver at Ryde was unaware of any cricket ground or that Hampshire were playing there. His office put him right and the 20-minute drive through rolling terrain calmed my impatience. Arrival at the Newclose ground also cheered me. It was a charming place, like the island a throwback to gentler times. It may not have been Antigua, but it would do nicely. This was the first time since 1962 that first-class cricket had been played on the island and though the cricket ground had been developed – most notably in the shape of a large and elegant wooden-framed pavilion – little else had in the surrounding area.

That was part of the appeal of the place. Vikki and I had been on holiday here some 10 years earlier, pootling and pottering around the 150 square miles for four days, having brought the car over on a ferry. We enjoyed long lunches and dinners, sitting atop cliffs and gazing out to sea. At the Needles, she told me of her time crewing for Ben Ainslie during the Round the Island Race for a feature article and being becalmed for hours without winds to drive the boat.

She had put her foot down, I remember, when I said that – having grown up in the seaside resort of Weymouth – I wanted to wander around Ryde. It was tacky, she said. Only after her death did I find pictures of her as a small girl in Ryde with her parents. Tackiness was part of the experience, I countered. We argued, but only teasingly, about our respective home towns, bickering as couples comfortable with themselves do. I guess she might have had unhappy childhood memories of Ryde and perhaps being told she couldn't have an ice cream.

By the end of our break together, we were laughing at the memory of a line from a radio show by John Shuttleworth (a creation of the Sheffield comedian Graham Fellows) about him and his wife Mary on a holiday to Whitby. "We ended up walking the cliffs again as we'd run out of things to do," he'd recalled.

The cricket field itself was in a bowl with a high bank on one side where a huge marquee looked down. I had decided to treat myself. For £60, I would receive a bacon roll and coffee breakfast, a light lunch and afternoon tea in this marquee, as well as seating outside it. It seemed a pretty good deal to me, especially given that sixty quid barely bought you a cheap seat at a Premier League football match these days.

The bacon rolls were late but nobody really minded. This was a club cricket set-up, being overseen by the Hampshire administration, and people were enjoying the simplicity and novelty of it all. It was a pleasure to be in such a setting after the longest, hardest of winters. I plonked myself on a chair, crossword to hand, and looked forward to the day.

It had plenty of attractions, after all, such as the England pace man Stuart Broad opening the bowling for Nottinghamshire, with Hampshire having won the toss and deciding to bat. It was one of the beauties of cricket. Unlike football, you could see such a towering figure of the game performing competitively in the humblest of venues in a top-class fixture. Broad was wayward, however, on a wicket that should have offered the bowlers something, and by lunch the Hampshire openers Oli Soames and Joe Weatherley had put on 85 without loss.

After an acceptable salmon fillet with new potatoes and salad, and the pleasant company of an Essex couple with a holiday home on the island and two Southampton-based cricket lovers who thought the crowd of over 1,000 more than the Ageas Bowl headquarters might host on a first morning, it was time for a stroll.

County "outgrounds" – that is, those grounds counties play at away from their HQ – are sadly rare these days, rare enough to have been captured in a sumptuous, nostalgic picture book that Vikki had bought me for Christmas one year, knowing my fondness for the game's geography. Sussex no longer played at Hastings, for example, nor Hampshire at Bournemouth. (I recall once covering Hampshire v Yorkshire at Dean Park for *The Guardian* in the 1980s, when two elderly women in the pavilion began berating Geoffrey Boycott for some slow batting as he came up the steps of the pavilion at the tea interval. "Gangway, please," replied the old curmudgeon. Honestly.)

Part of an outground's appeal is accessibility and absence of formality and I resolved to take advantage, to walk completely around the perimeter unhindered. There had been no bag searches at start of day (terrorism not having much of a history on the Isle of Wight, separatists being few and far between) and now no jobsworth blocked access.

Schoolboys and girls in uniform, given an afternoon off to attend on this day to remember, mingled with families. Cricket buffs abounded but there were also curious locals keen to see what had been talked about on the island, even if my taxi driver was out of the loop. This bucolic scene, with a new form of the game The Hundred – 100 balls per side – scheduled for city clamour, may not have been the future of cricket but there was surely nothing wrong with stepping back into the past for a while.

I found a deckchair at one end behind the bowler's arm and began to consider how fortunate I was now to be able to take in days like these, to be able to afford to. And then a guilt assailed me; V had been dead less than four months and here I was, feeling peaceful and content. I had no right.

And so I did what came naturally. I sabotaged the peace and contentment, began to feel anxious, frightened indeed. But it was not just about the prospect of life without Vikki. It was the prospect of my own life now being in question.

The cancer that had been detected in me in 2009, two years after Vikki's, had begun in my prostate. It was a family burden. Though my father did not die of it (smoking, the dust of building sites and emphysema caused that), he fell victim to it, as did three of his four brothers. When it came to mine, despite radiotherapy, involving seven weeks of daily treatment driving up to London though with weekends off, it reappeared in 2012 and spread into my pelvic lymph nodes.

At one point, Vikki and I were on the same drug, one that suppressed the oestrogen in women and testosterone in men on which breast and prostate cancers can feed. It produced hot flushes in us both and we would urge them to coincide on cold winter nights in bed to warm us both. They rarely did. More normally we would annoy each other with their timing, one throwing a duvet off while the other shivered.

Come the early April two months after Vikki's death, the blood test for my six-monthly check-up revealed that the cancer might well be on the move again. My PSA level (Prostate Specific Antogen – the guide, if not the definitive yardstick, for calibrating the seriousness of prostate cancer) had trebled and, while it was still comparatively low, it was a sign that something was not right. In fact, a scan – twice postponed, as if the tension needed increasing any more at this raw time – revealed that more pelvic lymph nodes were now affected. The Royal Marsden urologists said they would try me on another drug for a couple of months to see how I responded. There were plenty more options, they told me, if this didn't work – tablets and/or chemotherapy.

The thing at this time was that I wasn't sure if I wanted any of them. V was gone. What was left? Life frequently seemed so pointless these days. Where was the pleasure, where the hope? I had women friends I could lunch with, or even go to the theatre with, but I was never going to fall in love again, never going to find another partner. I was destined to live on my own, without the love of my life, without my soulmate – a word I had shied away from but which now seemed to apply better the longer time without her went on. We loved sport, similar music, books, films, theatre and galleries, the latter two Vikki having introduced me to.

I had felt similarly forlorn watching football on TV. I just could not get worked up any more about who won or who lost, whether it was a penalty or not. That was emasculation for a sports journalist who had thrived on such contrived debate and controversy throughout a 45-year career. Even here, now with cricket, I felt unengaged by the action and suddenly, in the afternoon lull, the utter so-whattery of it all consumed me, even though I was witnessing a good contest between bat and ball.

Of course, there were glimpses of pleasure in life; the ones I had tried to cling on to through Vikki's dying days: completing a crossword, hearing something funny on Radio 4. (Was it me, however, or were the comedy commissioners responsible for there being less that was funny on lately?) And tea and cake in the marquee with the fellow cricket lovers at my table to interrupt my melancholy was a comfort. What choice but to smile, to engage in conversation about which county was gaining the upper hand?

The day grew cold as play wound down, Hampshire working their way to a respectable 280 for six that would, in hindsight, prove a strong foundation. I rang my taxi driver of the morning, and within 15 minutes he arrived to take me to the hotel I had booked. Where else could it be but the Seaview, just a few miles along the coast from Ryde?

It all came back to me as I checked in at their small porthole reception. Vikki, yet again with her brilliant way based on taste and research, had found this place for our holiday those years ago. It was simple but classy (the latter word I could always hear V saying with a flat vowel as if sending herself up) and my little room was cosy and cute. I was just in need of a single now. The whole scene, evoking our past, made me smile and choke back a tear in turn.

I still could not face dinner alone, sitting there with people – if they were at all interested – staring at this lonely figure who was pretending to be occupied with what was on his phone. I had already done two crosswords that day. I couldn't sit there doing a third. I decided on a walk around the village, its one shop closed. Around the corner from the hotel, there was a view across the water to Portsmouth, with its distinctive Spinnaker Tower. I sat there for a while remembering, as I recognised this location we had both shared once together, and shedding yet more tears. Back in my room, I tried not to get panicky about being so far away from home, so far away from Vikki's memory and enduring presence in our home.

Come breakfast time, I was good and ready for a proper cooked meal, certainly hungry enough to endure any gaze directed at the singleton. Or, more accurately, the widower. At my table were two red roses in a thin vase. I could only smile. When she was alive, on most Fridays I would buy two long-stemmed roses for our living room. Since her death, I had continued the ritual but now bought four of them. There were the two for me to gaze on in our home from my armchair, and two for her grave.

Originally I thought I would watch three days of the cricket (with a fourth day always doubtful, given green wickets and the British weather) and indeed a while back I had booked two nights at the hotel, planning to get a hovercraft home after close of play on the third. Sussex and the opening fixture had been chastening for me, however, and I had cancelled the second night. I wanted to be back home, back at the place that bore her imprint.

And I had business in London. I had come up with the idea of a Vikki Orvice Book Prize, with a guarantee to ensure the publication of a female author's football book. Women in Football had agreed to endorse it. A judging panel had met and we had agreed a winner. Tonight was the announcement. I caught the hovercraft back across the water and picked up my car at Southsea.

It was a wonderful evening, a celebration of people fulfilling pledges in the organisation's #WhatIf campaign, which in my publishing company's case was: "What if we published a book by a female sports author?" The irony of "what if" was not lost on me. I had been asking myself the same question many times since Vikki died. What if I'd gone on more holidays with her? What if we'd got married sooner? And so on. Tonight, though, was about the uplifting rather than the downcast. It was a pleasure to announce as the winner a powerful book by an American writer, Susie Petruccelli, *Raised A Warrior*, about growing up as a then-rare female soccer fan in the US and playing for Harvard University. It pipped a fine memoir by the TV presenter Alison Bender.

Uplifting but tiring, too. Putting on a brave face is hard work and tiring. The recounted memories of Vikki on the night by women who had known her well were touching. For each crumb of comfort at what had been, however, there was a slice of sadness at what was gone. It was a strange feeling: wanting to get away, to be alone with that sadness, but at the same time knowing that it was going to be even more painful on my own, surrounded no longer by kind, supportive souls.

Over the next few days, I kept an eye on what was taking place on the Isle of Wight. Hampshire would fall to 310 all out on the second morning, which seemed a mediocre score until they bowled Nottinghamshire out for 239. The Hampshire captain Sam Northeast and Ajinkya Rahane, the Indian Test batsman spending a couple of months as the county's overseas player, both then made centuries as Notts were set 438 to win. They would limp to 194 all out, a defeat of 244 runs and an early-season indication of the travails that would beset them as summer unfolded.

It was a win that would set Hampshire up well for the 50-over, Royal London Cup final they had reached, to be played at Lord's against Somerset. Yes, a one-day Cup final before the end of May in a season that was being reconfigured due to the six-week-long World Cup in England.

I noted there were tickets available still for the one-day final, possibly due to the early stage of the season – though it was seven weeks old, it was not yet ingrained in the nation's sporting psyche – and possibly because it was being contested by two of the counties without big-city support. I resolved to go. It was a weekend, and not just any old weekend. It was going to mark my and Vikki's ninth wedding anniversary. (It had only taken us just the 15 years after meeting to get married.) I needed to do something different, after all, given the weekends I had been suffering. Several people have been credited with the saying, though it is Einstein who is probably best remembered for it: "The definition of insanity is doing the same thing over and over again and expecting a different result."

Whatever the uncertainty about who said it, I knew that what I had begun to experience a month after Vikki died, and which had the potential still to overwhelm me, most certainly felt like insanity.

·7·

March Madness

· · · · · · · · · · · · · · · · · · ·

In America in early spring, they play the college basketball finals, when all the universities, big and small, come together in a manic knockout tournament. It is magnificent but it is mad. In fact they call it March Madness. And March madness is what happened with me and to me in the wake of Vikki's death.

Now, what follows in this chapter was dark, painful and terrifying for me. It may trigger echoes for other people too, though we are all different. What unnerves me may not unnerve you and vice versa. But so many people are troubled by echoes of their past resurfacing when they are emotionally vulnerable, as I was now – not that I knew it at the time, which was part of the problem. I became irrationally riddled with anxiety and had no understanding why. So, as they say on the news before they announce the football results, if you don't want to know, look away now.

It all started with the most beautiful picture of Vikki I had ever seen, the one that appears at the front of this book.

The funeral had been 10 days before and my daughter Alex had now gone back to Singapore. I was at home alone for the weekend and at a loose end. I mooched and meandered around the house. I stared at some of Vikki's clothes – the last outfit she wore – still draped on the chair in our bedroom. I couldn't even contemplate moving them, nor any of the clothes in her wardrobes. I did think, briefly, about claiming some of the chest-of-drawers space – she had three to my one – but the reality of doing even that provoked an anxiety in me. It would feel like I was getting over this too soon – not that I saw any way of getting over these intense feelings just now.

(I hate the terms "moving on" and "closure", by the way. Life may go on, and new, different times will arrive, but "moving on" suggests leaving something behind; "closure" suggests an end to things. I never wanted – want – to move on from Vikki's memory, nor do I expect my feelings for her to come to any sort of "closure".)

In my unease, I wandered into V's office. This was her space, a reflection of her. When she was alive, I came in only to supply her with tea and cake, to use her printer or to ask her something. Its contents, in drawers and filing cabinets, were a mystery to me and even when she was away working, I felt no desire to intrude.

I looked at the whole shelf of my books she had saved. She always got the first copy, signed with a personal message from me, usually thanking her for her support. I smiled. On another shelf, there was something – a couple of things – I did find easy to throw out: some books written by a previous boyfriend of hers, containing affectionate dedications. My insecure reaction would presage plenty more of it.

After that, I looked fondly at the framed pictures on the wall of her with various sports stars, from David Beckham and Kevin Keegan to Paula Radcliffe and Seb Coe. Hung proudly on the wall was a page from a Sheffield United match-day programme that featured her. I sat in her chair, at her desk. And I cried. It didn't take much. I was a tap that needed little turning.

Now I became curious about all she had accumulated down the years. After all, I was spending my days thinking about her, and any conversations I was having with other people were all about her. This was another way of reconnecting with her.

The top drawer of her filing cabinet contained old school exercise books and university essays. She loved school, she had told me, and had thrived at Leicester. She was what an entitled old Etonian who wanted rewards without the work might have described as a girly swot.

The next drawer contained her favourite cuttings of stories she had written. Gold-medal moments, notably Super Saturday at London 2012 when she had the back page lead and Jess Ennis, Mo Farah and Greg Rutherford had all won gold for Great Britain in 45 minutes. They had all sent her video messages of support, which made her cry, in the latter stages of her illness. There were, too, big interviews with such as Usain Bolt, ghostwritten columns with Ian Wright and Rebecca Adlington. And an amazing exclusive she had secured early on in her time at *The Sun* when an agent had secretly supplied her with the full details of Alan Shearer's contract when he joined Newcastle United.

After that, in drawer three, various personal papers – letters of appointment to her old newspapers, herograms from editors and bosses among them – and stationery.

Then trouble began when I opened drawer four.

It contained wallet after wallet of photographs, maybe 2,000 snaps in total, going back to when she was a teenager. Who could have resisted going through them? Certainly not this person who knew her best – or thought he did – and loved her most. That last bit he was sure of. The photos had been there for many years, clearly, but I had never seen them before.

I sifted through. Some made me smile, of her having fun times in the days before I met her. Near the top of the pile was that photo of her looking up into a camera, chin resting on her palm. Her hair was jet black, her eyes alight. Her smile enveloped the picture. It was V encapsulated in one shot. I loved it. I took my own photo of it on my phone and it became my screen saver.

But it began to niggle me… I hadn't taken this picture. Hadn't been there when it was taken. It was clearly from a time when we were together, but I didn't remember it. So who had taken it?

I found the actual roll of film in the wallet, along with the contact sheet. That sheet showed that this was the end of a roll. There was just one more photo after it – a blurry one that presumably Vikki had thrown away as it was nowhere to be found. I was part intrigued, part agitated. I had to know more. And so, after a weekend of wondering and worrying, I took the roll of film to be developed just to see if that final, blurry, picture told me any more. To my dismay, it was going to take a week.

Naturally, I didn't let it go there. The other pictures in the wallet revealed this to be from late 2004, after Vikki had come back from the Athens Olympics. There were pictures of her at a Kelly Holmes mentoring scheme in South Africa on the same roll. I remembered her going on that press trip but couldn't remember when it was.

So how did I find that out? By doing something I should never have done, but – in hindsight – needed to do. It would touch my open wounds, pour petrol on the bonfire of my pain. This at a time when Vikki had been dead just over a month, a time that also prompted something agonising for me.

You know how it is with your partner. If you're honest, you quite look forward to a bit of time on your own when they go away for a while. It was attractive to have control of the TV remote, to leave socks lying around, to eat a bit of junk food, not to be chided for dishes left in the sink.

Whenever we were separated for longer periods, though, such as when she went to a major athletics championship or the Olympic Games, or I went to a World

Cup, we would be missing each other badly after a month or so and both be desperate to reconnect. That also happened, to be honest, in some early, tricky and turbulent, times of our relationship. After a month apart, perhaps as a result of some serious argument, one of us could just not resist contacting the other. Now, obvious as it was, the reality hit home that this was simply never going to happen again. She was not physically there to be reconnected with. The finality brought a feeling to my stomach of not so much butterflies as Rugby League players going hammer and tongs at each other.

In the week waiting for the photos to be developed, I couldn't resist exploring more of the pictures in the bottom drawer of Vikki's filing cabinet. They went back years, to long before we met. Among them were plenty of her on holiday with her previous boyfriends, portraits she had taken of those men. They provoked in me a gnawing jealousy that grew and grew into a green monster.

I'm sure Vikki had not wanted me to find them. Indeed, in a notebook on her desk was a to-do list that said: "Sort out photo drawer." It remained without a line through it. As with much, time had beaten her.

I didn't just look at the photos, I pored over them obsessively. Never before seen – isn't that a line used to pique fascination? Here she was before I had met her, in her twenties and early thirties on holidays, at weddings and family functions, simply out with friends. She looked amazing; so vivacious, so attractive.

She dressed beautifully too. That was always the key to my Vikki; while she was capable of competing in the then male-dominated world of sports journalism and was seen almost as one of the boys by many colleagues, she was determined not to become some kind of tomboy, some honorary bloke. She was a feminist, and feminine too. She liked to wear well-cut dresses, have expensive haircuts, so that she would not just be defined as a professional but as a woman too.

It was part of the medley of contrasts and aspects of Vikki that so chimed with me, touched my soul. She was intensely bright but not especially practical; she was thoughtful and pensive, but garrulous and passionate; tough but soft. They were things not evident in pictures unless you knew her well, for her looks mirrored her personality. Once I pointed it out, she always preferred to be photographed from the left, which was her prettier side. She looked tougher from the right.

From the filing cabinet to her desk drawers. Another step I should never have taken but could not resist doing in my need to know more and stay close to her. The bottom one contained pocket diaries from the last 30 years, more calendars with appointments in them rather than any journal content. They went back to the early 1990s before I knew her, then to times when our relationship was on and off for a while. They contained dinner dates with various men, some professional, but also some personal. Some of them she later told me about, as she did about that football manager who had asked her out, and as at least three other journalists had. (She would also tell me later about the well-known figure in the athletics world who once hit on her during a time when we were living together but before we got married.)

Even in my agitated state of worrying about whether I knew everything behind these photos and these diary entries, I knew Vikki had done nothing wrong. She had just lived her life without knowing what or whom the future held for her. That wasn't the issue here. The issue was me, the issues mine. Except that I had no grasp of them beyond the brutality of acknowledging that she wasn't there for me to ask questions of, to seek needy reassurances from.

And except for one feeling I recognised vividly: shame. It is the curse of the using addict and the burden of the one in recovery. I felt ashamed of my reaction to what would not for many people be a concern. The past was the past, and all that. But this was furiously evoking echoes of things that had happened to me long ago. For now, I could not understand what. I just knew something was seriously spooking me.

Whatever was happening, to sadness was now coming the madness. I had been dipping into Joan Didion's book *The Year of Magical Thinking*, in which she nailed grief with its unexpected set of feelings that stretch into the distance well beyond the sheer agony at the loss of a lover. This was exactly how I was feeling just now: "Nor can we know ahead of the fact (and here lies the heart of the difference between grief as we imagine it and grief as it is) the unending absence that follows, the void, the very opposite of meaning, the relentless succession of moments during which we will confront the experience of meaningless itself."

Consumed by that need of the writer to detail her experience of losing her husband, her book told of a year in which she felt a compulsion to discover exactly how and when he had died. There was a death certificate, of course, outlining a heart attack as the cause, but she wanted – needed – answers to her questions of where and when. Before the ambulance got him to hospital? In the hospital?

It mirrors the experience of so many, such as those poor family members whose loved ones die in hospital or abroad, well away from their presence. It is painful seeing them on television almost blaming themselves, or at least feeling they could or should have done something more. I now understood the tragically bereaved on the news programmes after deaths of children lost abroad, or of hospital errors, demanding answers. Once I might uncharitably have thought that answers weren't going to bring the person back and they should just get over it. How little did I know.

Forensically, Joan Didion set about getting responses to her questions and, in my heightened state of anxiety, I needed some too. Who had taken that gorgeous picture of V, for starters? It was clearly captured by someone with a lot of love for her. As somebody once said to me, quoting what a photographer had told them: "You always take better pictures of those you love." I had stopped using the photo as the screen saver on my phone as soon as I realised that I hadn't taken it, that it had been captured by someone who, I thought in my distressed state, might have been in love with her, and that this had been an intimate dinner.

It dawned on me that the timeline of Vikki's life before we met was hazy to me. I sort of knew about all her previous jobs, flats and relationships but had never really grasped how they fitted together. Now I was inflamed by a desire to join the dots, put all in its proper order. To know everything about her.

I rang her friends and the colleagues she was close to. I asked them all manner of questions, about her and her life, right from the time she went to university. I invited a few to my – our – home, made arrangements to go and stay with some of them for a couple of days so we could talk and I could build my picture. A couple of days away was all I could manage still before I felt the urge to get home, where the memories of Vikki were richest for me.

One of her close friends dating back to university offered to come and see me on a Saturday and we spent eight hours just talking, she illuminating me about V as a student and their contact and confidences ever since. It was early evening before we knew it. God, there was so much to talk about when it came to Vikki. Her life had been crammed, both with experiences and people.

The photos came back from the developers. In the one that was blurry, taken after the lovely shot of her, I could make out St Paul's Cathedral in the background. I had a thought about where it might be and, checking their website, and pictures of their dining room, I could confirm this was indeed the restaurant by the Thames I had guessed. I remembered her telling me she had had dinner there once or twice with an old friend and colleague who had been at our wedding with his partner. I rang him. He didn't recall taking the picture but he did remember having dinner with her there around that time as he worked nearby. I was relieved. I calmed down. For now. The way I was, however, meant this agitation wasn't going to go away any time soon. Soon I was back to the ritual of going to bed, listening to the radio and doing a crossword, then suffering from night sweats and terrors as soon as I turned out the light, lying awake and shaking for hour upon hour. I couldn't concentrate to read. Podcasts helped.

Over the next month, I travelled to more of her friends, our friends, and questioned them to the point that they were clearly worried about me and my obsessiveness. I think I was placed on suicide watch by the kindly people in the village who had helped organise Vikki's funeral. This wasn't just about my grief. This was something altogether freakier, less recognisable – to me as well as them.

Not that I felt it to be all sinister. I simply wanted to know more about the woman I loved. What was she like – beyond what she had told me – when she was a teenager, 25, 30?

I first met Vikki in the press box at Selhurst Park in the earlyish 1990s, when she was in her early thirties. I think it may have been May 1992 and Wimbledon, then ground-sharing with Crystal Palace, against her revered Sheffield United. She was covering the game for the *Daily Mail*, I was on *The Observer*. I thought she was attractive (and I registered the black leather jacket and smart jeans) but thought little more of it when she told me she was engaged. (Why did she tell me that? A bit forward.) It was not until four years later, her by now on *The Sun*, when we first became an item.

Some of the questions about her teenage years were answered by the proper diaries, journals, of those years that I found in another chest in the house that had not been opened for years and whose contents I wondered about. They were touching and amusing rather than worrying to me. They contained a lot of comment about academic school work, dark poems, and occasional snippets about snogging a boy in town after a few illicit drinks before throwing up on him.

Friends indulged me and my questioning. I look back with thanks. As is vital for the bereaved, they gave me space to share about V and the times we'd had. They never looked bored though they must have tired of my intensity. They told me too about her past life and why her previous relationships had not worked out. At one point, in a rare healthy moment, I found myself grateful that those liaisons had not lasted. She would never have been interested in me if they had. We would never have ended up together.

It took a while before we properly committed to each other – actually, to be honest, before I committed properly to her, as her friends always insisted how devoted to me she was. It didn't even go smoothly after my separation then divorce from my first wife, hence the on–off times, when, one of her best friends told me, her dinner dates with other men were simply designed to make me jealous. They worked. And it took way too long for us to get married.

Thus did I go into a funk of regrets and what ifs. I punished myself emotionally. What if I'd committed sooner? We'd have had more time together, wasted less of it. As well as regret, anger consumed me. Looking at those pictures of her in her twenties, with then boyfriends and at all those occasions and times when she appeared so happy, even allowing for the fact that people always smile in photos, I had a gnawing sense of feeling cheated. I envied those times they'd had with her in her youth.

The last years with Vikki had been difficult physically, and frequently painful emotionally, as both our bodies deteriorated, hers more quickly than mine, due to our cancers. It had been, simply and largely, a struggle for survival. And I was having a struggle to recall those happy times of ours, when we had been fit and well.

Sure, we had good memories these past few years, of holidays particularly, and little times together such as at concerts at the Royal Festival Hall or plays at the National Theatre, along with sporting events together; watching Salisbury FC, where I was vice-chairman, grow again after I'd helped to rebuild the club, seeing Sheffield United promoted from League One. But my abiding memory at this time was of the body cowed by her illness and of me the anxious figure trying haplessly to help, nurture and support her. Where were those two figures of 20 years ago, so energetic, so full of life? At times I raged in the privacy of the house. As well as the 23 years I'd had with her, greedily I wanted those times that those men had had with her too.

And people kept talking of her wide smile, of it being her trademark. Well, it was certainly part of the package that attracted me to her – I loved her big teeth and generous mouth – but I had overlooked its impact, while it had made a huge impression on others, in these past few years. I felt guilty that I hadn't noticed more of late her special qualities that the obituaries and tributes to her noted. But then, when you are part of a couple, the daily routine is about just living. In our case, it was also about just living with cancer. Maybe it was a compliment to me that she didn't need to present her "specialness" to me, that she trusted me with her failings and foibles too. In good moments, I would probably be happy that we took each other for granted, that we were familiar enough with each other not to need to pretend or be on best behaviour and to just be comfortable together. But that is hindsight's kindness. These were not good moments.

Above all, overwhelmingly and achingly, what I wanted was to start again. For us to meet when young and cancer-free, for us to have had children together. For us to know then what we knew in our later years, how crazy about each other we were and so not to worry about any consequences of that love. Instead of wasting time, just to give in to our feelings when we both knew, during our times apart – those missing month-long periods – that we were never going to get over each other, get each other out of the other's mind or system.

What I wanted was us to be able to make consuming love together as healthy people again, as she had with those lucky enough to have had relationships with her before I met her. Even if only for one last time. My memories now, clouded by illness and death, just could not access a time when we did.

I remembered us watching together a few years earlier an American TV drama called *The Affair*, in which Dominic West and Ruth Wilson have just that. They too go through agonies before they finally give in to their feelings and commit. At one point he, Noah, says to her: "I knew there would never be any peace until we were together." She, Alison, said she knew that too.

I turned to Vikki at the end of the scene and said, "You know, that's exactly how I felt about you." She looked at me and replied across the room: "I felt the same." I develop goosebumps as I write that. And then feel a regret that too often we sat on opposite sides of the room when watching television, me probably watching football on my laptop, instead of cuddling up together with the dramas and movies that she liked.

Now I found I could watch little on TV that we watched together, such as the odd soap and drama, or *University Challenge*, in which she was very competitive. When I checked what was saved on the TV planner, I found there was no space on it. It was taken up by multiple episodes of shows she had watched for comfort in her dying days, such as *Location, Location, Location*.

In the immediate aftermath of Vikki's death, I had felt a relief for her that a deterioration that was so cruel for such an active woman was over, along with the end of my stressed caring. Then in the weeks around the funeral I had experienced a mixture of numbness and sadness, both for her curtailed life – at 56. 56? What the fuck? – and also my loneliness. It prompted frequent outbursts of sobbing that struck at any time and anywhere. In the street or a shop, I could often conceal my tears. Only in the privacy of the house did I give vent to the full force of them. The numbness meant that I could deal with writing and delivering her eulogy without breaking down. It was also, I decided, about her and not me and I owed it to her then not to collapse.

Now I was just pissed off. With her. With the situation. She had left me. Of course she hadn't left me on purpose, nor clearly had she wanted to, but the stark fact remained that she had. I was now alone, enduring secondary cancer myself. I had looked after her. Now I had nobody to do that in return for me. The prospect of falling ill alone, especially having seen the deficiencies in an underfunded NHS, away from the Marsden, and in inundated A&E departments alarmed me. And I projected, during my wakeful nights, that I could well die alone.

This whole cocktail of internal chaos was with me every day but would intensify on a Saturday, the day I had discovered the photos and diaries. In such a state, I would see on Twitter a line saying "Vikki Orvice follows" of the person posting a tweet and would momentarily misunderstand and hastily go to V's Twitter feed to see if she had posted something. Sometimes, I thought about phoning her mobile to see what would happen. (I did hear on the radio a story of a woman doing that with her late husband's phone. Somebody answered, the number having been reassigned to that person, and they became friends.)

And so, one weekend, unable to face another episode of the madness that would see me obsessing about V's past and who might have been in it and when, I decided to try something different. I booked on a one-day course near Cambridge on crime writing hosted by Sophie Hannah, the celebrated thriller writer whom Vikki had once booked and interviewed for our village book festival that V co-founded. I headed for the countryside writer's retreat and found respite and company for a few hours. Sophie remembered Vikki and our village church well, offered me her sympathies. She wondered what I was going to do now with my life. I hadn't thought about it at all, I said. I was still unable to contemplate life, a future, without V. Sophie said she had just become course director for a new crime-writing Masters degree at Cambridge University for part-time students. Why didn't I consider applying? It sounded interesting. I said I would think about it, grateful that my interest in something had been stimulated.

During one fitful sleep around this time, some six weeks after Vikki's death, I dreamt of V for the first time. In it, I was on a course and clearing up all my papers at the end of the day, before getting in my car to drive home. I found her running a local coffee shop. I couldn't see her at first. She was behind a counter, wearing familiar blue trousers and a blue blouson she liked. I asked her how she was. She didn't reply but she had a pained look on her face. And then the dream was over.

What did it mean? I had no idea, but it was indicative of my desperation to reconnect with her. To see her again, even if only one last time. To have her beside me in bed again to cuddle into her back, she into mine. To ask her the questions. To join the dots. To wake up from a sleep and find that moment of relief when you realise that the dark dreamscape wasn't reality. But it was.

I met for coffee with a friend around this time and told her of this. She in turn told me how she had lost her mother some time earlier. Then, each time she was in a certain shop, she would find her mother standing alongside her, giving her advice about, for example, what curtains to buy.

"What, like a ghost?" I asked.

"No. Literally her. Standing alongside me, talking to me. And I would answer back. We would have a conversation."

It went on, she added, for a couple of years before it stopped. The woman concerned thought it ended when both parties were ready to let go of each other.

My initial reaction was not that my friend was a nutter. She was a sane, professional woman of high achievement and I had no fears for her sanity, unlike mine. No, I was jealous. I would have given anything for Vikki to appear alongside me, for us to have a conversation. Indeed, I almost willed it. Our house was 400 years old and my daughter, when staying, would sometimes say that she sensed a spiritual presence in the bedroom she would sleep in. Alex was sensitive to these things. Recalling this, some nights I would sit on the landing for long stretches in the dark, a duvet around me, hoping that Vikki's spectre would somehow emerge from her office, the door of which I left open. We'd both liked the film *Ghost*, me largely because Demi Moore has the same haircut in it as Vikki favoured. Sadly, V never showed up. In visual form, anyway. I laugh at myself now as I write this but when I used to come home sometimes and see that pictures on the wall seemed a little askew, as if they had moved, I did wonder. Then I realised that the cleaners had been that day.

While I never understood this concept that denial was a stage of grief – how the heck could you not realise the person was dead? – I was almost refusing to believe that I was never going to see her again nor hear her voice again. I guess that is why people go to mediums. It was weird. I would regularly go to her grave – still a mess of mud with just a wooden cross – to take flowers, just to be near her. There she was, in the ground, just six feet beneath my shoes but light years away.

The majority of those trusted people I did share (some of) this with, suggested to me that a lot of it was normal, that it was part of the grieving process. I wasn't going nuts, just mourning. How could any of this be normal though? I'd just lost my wife, for pity's sake, and while family loss may be happening all around, all day, it hadn't happened to me before. I really didn't want this to be normal.

And I don't think, actually, that several close to me did believe my jealousy and obsessive investigation into

Vikki's past, to be normal. Fewer still understood it. To be honest, nor did I. I just didn't know at this point how to extract myself from that jealousy and obsession triggered by the diaries and photos. And with that cocktail of feelings would come another bout of draining shame that I should be emotionally healthier, better than all this yukky stuff after so many years of recovery from addiction.

Little things sustained me in moments of painful panic, slogans I had learned in Alcoholics Anonymous such as "one day at a time", of course, and "this too shall pass". But while I never thought I would drink again, I began to question everything else. Would it pass? Really? It felt there was no way that this was ever going to go away. After all, she was gone for ever.

Being a people-pleaser sometimes and always very British in my fear of attracting unwelcome attention, in public and in daylight I was mostly plausible – apart from odd moments, such as the time I burst into tears in a bank and a member of staff sat me down and fetched me some water. Indeed, quite a few people would tell me how well they thought I was doing. In private, alone, it didn't feel that way. On top, it was at that time when I'd discovered that as well as my mental health and emotional well-being deteriorating, my physical health was too.

After that blood test which revealed that my PSA had tripled since my last check-up four months earlier,

I really didn't need the added uncertainty and stress in my life provoked by having the scan postponed twice, due to a shortage of the dye they needed to inject to show up any spread of the disease. In fact, I got shirty with the Marsden and urged them to speed this up. I had learned much from Vikki about fighting for rights, rather than being passive, when confronted by organisations, no matter how benign they were. Finally it took place.

Then came a week of wondering. To be honest, I wasn't really worrying. I was actually thinking that if my cancer had spread, it might be a sign, and one for the best. I could decline any more treatment and let the disease take its course. I had been dubious anyway about whether life was worth continuing with, hadn't I?

After all, one Bible-black Saturday night into Sunday morning I'd even googled "Painless ways to die by suicide", thinking there might be a quick pill I could take, as you see in the movies, rather than some traumatic messy event (for others, family and strangers who have to witness or deal with its aftermath) such as throwing oneself under a train. It seemed there was no such thing as a pain-free suicide, however. Even pills can be long, slow and agonising. I was probably fortunate at that time, though, that I could never be bothered to go beyond page two of a Google search. These days, in the cause of prevention, all the articles about it being a bad idea are at the top.

Yes, cancer's worst was the best way out, it seemed to me. Natural. And if there was any shred of truth in my religion, I would be reunited with Vikki. Now, that I would welcome. If it meant I would be with her again, in some kind of glorious afterlife, bring it on.

After discovering that my cancer was now in more of the pelvic lymph nodes to where it had insinuated itself from the prostate seven years ago, I wanted a prognosis, unlike Vikki. One doctor was quite pessimistic, saying I had three to five years. Another was more optimistic, suggesting a minimum of five. I was offered a drug that they hoped would stabilise me and interrupt the spread. It was going to get me eventually, as, like Vikki, I had secondary, incurable cancer, but they could postpone it. And who knows what other treatment might be available in five years?

I asked my therapist. He told me to take it for now so that I could make better choices when more time had passed. I thought about Vikki. Having taken everything available and offered to her, so much did she cherish and cling to life, she would have been so angry with me had I refused treatment. I was suddenly ashamed of even contemplating not taking the drug. And so I began taking it. This particular one would probably work, I was told, for between nine and 24 months. After that, it would probably be chemotherapy. That, with all its brutality, would seem a better time to make a proper decision.

I mean, let alone making a major decision, I couldn't even decide what to cook that night. Or even whether I could be arsed to cook. There were so many things I couldn't do. It was also ironic that now I could go anywhere in the world I chose, with no one to answer to, and yet all I wanted was to be in our house where her presence, through objects and photographs, was everywhere. Other things I couldn't do? Still couldn't move the last clothes she wore from her chair in the bedroom, let alone touch those in her wardrobe, save to take an orange coat of hers and place it on a hook in the hallway so that I would see her favourite colour when I walked into the house.

I grew annoyed with myself, for losing my car and house keys, which would be in the fridge, or for overfilling my teacup or running out of dishwasher tablets and light bulbs. And when that anger became too much for me to bear, I communicated it to those closest to me. I so wanted my daughter home from Singapore that I put too much pressure on her and she grew upset, and fearful for me. Join the club. I was founder member of it. I was also fearful *of* me.

Then another old saying came into my head: if you do what you always did, you get what you always got. My time in AA had taught me that change was the only permanent thing in life, that we changed or drank again and died. And Vikki wouldn't have wanted me to die just yet, while the Marsden could keep me alive as they had her. It was time to do something to change the course of this juggernaut grief, even if I couldn't halt it in its tracks.

· 8 ·

One Day

· · · · · · · · · · ·

It was the imminent arrival of the May bank-holiday weekend that had convinced me it would be a good idea to buy two tickets for the Royal London Cup final at Lord's between Hampshire and Somerset. The word "weekend" provoked enough dread in me, let alone one with the adjective "long" in front of it.

While it was not Championship cricket, 100 overs in a day made for a proper match in which the full skills of the game, including just occupying the crease if needs be, came into play. It was certainly more than simply wellying it as hard and as often as possible, as the shorter Twenty20 form of the game seems to be. With batsmen needing to have some circumspection about running out of wickets and so pacing an innings, bowlers thus also had a bit of a chance of being more than cannon fodder. There was strategy. And strategy, in my view, should be a defining characteristic of cricket. I guess I had been spoiled by my experience of being assigned Mike Brearley's seminal book *The Art of Captaincy* to edit for serialisation when I was a sub-editor on *The Guardian*.

Lord's not being sold out also meant that for me the experience should be manageable. There should be space for my grief to breathe, rather than be enveloped by the claustrophobia of a crowd. And a companion would help, in the form of Seth Burkett, who had written a charming book – *The Boy In Brazil*, about life as a professional footballer for a small-town team in South America – that I had put out through my publishing company. It was also the weekend of mine and Vikki's ninth wedding anniversary and while I wanted to be at home on my own to respect and honour the date of 29 May, the echoes of recent painful Saturdays past added to the appeal of a day out.

Once, one-day cricket finals were the equivalent of the FA Cup final: fitting, exciting ends to the domestic season. They were memorable days, events and occasions, and schoolboys would grow up able to recite winners and years. (Sporty schoolgirls, Vikki informed me, did not retain the minutiae like blokes.) I could even remember sponsors; when I were a lad, it were the Gillette Cup. In the early days it was 65 overs a side. Imagine that: a potential 130 overs in a day. Then, with games finishing near dark, it became 60 overs before bigger hitting and slower over rates brought us to 50.

In Somerset's case, it was not too difficult to remember their one-day trophy wins. It took them until 1979 to succeed, with that rock and roll team that would ever stay in the memory: not just Ian Botham, Viv Richards and Joel Garner but Brian Rose, Peter "Dasher" Denning and Vic Marks too. Names I knew readily from the halcyon days of the 1970s and 1980s, unlike most Somerset cricketers today.

Was my lack of familiarity with them now more about me or the modern game? A bit of both, but mostly the latter, surely, because it was no longer on free-to-air television. Sky TV had been good for the game in pumping in money, no one could deny that, and that money helped counties to spend on grass-roots cricket and getting youngsters involved. There could be little doubt, however, that the best advertisement for the sport, and best attraction to it, was seeing the big games in the mainstream of public consciousness.

Somerset's opponents those 40 years ago, Northamptonshire, had had some hotshots too: Geoff Cook and Wayne Larkins as openers, Test players both, then more internationals in Allan Lamb and Peter Willey. Sarfraz Nawaz led the bowling attack. In the end, Richards had scored a century and Garner taken six wickets as Somerset won by 45 runs.

I had friends who were Somerset supporters, indeed had recruited me to play for a touring team for a few years who went by the name of Frome Innswingers. They featured three of the Dredges, brothers of Colin who bowled medium pace for Somerset in that era under the nickname of the Demon of Frome. They were a lively bunch, but then so was I in those days. The bars of cricket clubs in South Wales and Leicestershire were richer for our presence.

As a man of less hedonistic tastes these days, I was grateful that today Lord's was not bursting with people and excitement, as it had been back then. The tickets I had purchased were in the midst of the Somerset crowd, with a few raucous lads among them of the sort my old friends – some of them now teachers, even heads – used to be. Back then, Adge Cutler was sung lustily (my own old favourite line of his and his Wurzels being: "From Charterhouse to Cheddar, he's champion dung-spreader") and cider drunk liberally. If a little more restrained, tastes hadn't changed that much.

With large swathes of seats empty, it meant that we could move around if I was uncomfortable with the company and still find relative peace, if not quite the solitary spots of the four-day game. And closer to the bowler's arm. While that would have been unthinkable once, even harder to contemplate today was the fact that this was to be the last 50-over final at the "Home of Cricket", as it marketed itself these days, for the foreseeable future before a revamp of the competition the following season due to the scheduled arrival of The Hundred.

Unfortunately, to mark the occasion, the match turned out to be something of a damp squib on a chilly bank-holiday Saturday.

Hampshire won the toss and elected to bat. They were without their two England players, James Vince and Liam Dawson, who were involved with the national squad in a World Cup warm-up against Australia at Southampton. Vince's absence particularly meant that Hampshire struggled with the bat and they lost regular wickets. Stand-in captain Sam Northeast's half-century helped them to the respectability of 244 for eight at the end of their 50 overs.

If the match was to be competitive, their pace bowler Fidel Edwards had to pick up wickets; bowling Somerset out rather than containing them looked Hampshire's only hope. A 20-year-old opener by the name of Tom Banton was not to be cowed by Caribbean pace, however. Indeed, he accumulated 69 runs of savage elegance – in the sort of wave-creating innings that would see him selected for England's T20 series in New Zealand in the autumn and South Africa in the winter – and it was 20 overs before Hampshire could prise him out. James Hildreth then made an unbeaten 72 and Somerset were home with 39 balls to spare.

Once, with almost 500 runs scored, that might have seemed like a cracking day's play. Nowadays, it was a routine, mediocre match that can make the one-day game seem dull, as it cries out for close matches and thrilling finales.

Lord's sat and watched unenthralled, knowing that the result was foregone from about 20 overs into the Somerset innings, but remaining in situ because it was an early-summer Saturday of cricket and every last drop of daylight, when long winter's nights were to be contemplated, was to be savoured. Personally, I was still in my Saturday-night fearful state and the later home the better.

At the end, Somerset went through their champagne cork-popping celebrations against the sponsors' backdrops. These days, to this fuddy-duddy, celebrations in all sports seem contrived and choreographed for television rather than spontaneous. It used to rile referees that a "floor manager" at televised football matches was instructing them from the sidelines when they could allow the match to kick off. Now it was almost as if players had been told by the media people: "OK, everybody jump up now and go a bit bananas while the tickertape falls so that the camera crew and photographers can get those neatly composed images."

Still, even I couldn't begrudge Somerset their fun. After the class of '79, it had been another 22 years before they tasted victory again in a Lord's final. Their last trophy had been the T20 tournament of 2005.

Ah, that summer of 2005. Vikki was 42 and I was 50. It was the summer she went to Singapore to see London awarded the 2012 Olympic Games. It was the year I became chief football writer of the *Mail on Sunday*, my first assignment being to cover England on a tour of the United States. We had been only nine months in our new house together. I remember ringing her from New York, walking down Fifth Avenue, content, at ease, our life together finally settled. I remember telling her how blessed I felt. How much I loved her. She told me how much she loved me too.

That's where grief takes you. You're writing about a cricket match. About a pleasant enough day, even if it did peter out, on a nice enough evening, if one growing a little chilly, at the world's most celebrated cricket ground with the promise of warmer days and hotter games to come. And then, all of a sudden, comes a memory of her, of the two of you.

At first, you savour it, wrap yourself in the warmth it offers. Then comes the sadness, before the anger, at the realisation that such moments will never be repeated. That those instances of sharing with each other what was happening in our worlds were gone. That life is slipping away. Hers has already slipped away. Yours, old son, will not be too far behind.

There's a trite saying that urges people not to cry because it's over but to smile because it happened. We're all supposed to nod at its wisdom and try to apply it to our own situation. That Saturday night, as with every Saturday night since March, coming back to our empty house, I gazed at the long-stemmed roses in our living room I had bought the day before and had to acknowledge that there was no getting away from the tears, nor from the reality that my life as it had been was over.

Our wedding anniversary was four days away. Sad as it might feel, I couldn't just wallow on that day, I thought, despite wallowing being acceptable at times and even unavoidable. I owed it to her to honour our life together on that special day of the year. The fact that she had agreed to marry me, had chosen to spend her life with me, needed to be celebrated.

·9·

These Foolish Things

The sun shone brightly on our wedding day, a fitting start to what would be almost nine perfect years of marriage after 15 of smooth unwedded union. And if you believe that, you'll believe anything.

Actually, it chucked it down. From early morning until about half an hour after the service in our village church where her funeral was also conducted. It was only then that the photographer, a lovely man by the name of Mike King – a colleague on *The Observer*, who also died too young, aged 52, in 2015 – could get some shots without umbrellas in them. There were some lovely pictures of Vikki in full bridal regalia walking the 100 yards from our house to the church, carrying a brolly adorned with sunflower images and red wellington boots.

Now, on Monday 29 May, on what would have been our ninth wedding anniversary, I took the wedding album out from a cupboard and slowly savoured it all again. The memories, to paraphrase a line written by Aaron Sorkin for James Earl Jones in *Field of Dreams*, came so thick that I had to brush them away from my face.

First, I recalled the night I proposed to her. We were on an autumn holiday in the Lake District and had just enjoyed a good dinner at a lovely hotel. I had been thinking about asking her for a while and now, as we enjoyed coffee in a deserted, warm lounge, seemed like a good opportunity.

"I've been thinking," I said. "Would you like to get married?"

She was leafing through a magazine and barely looked up.

"I suppose I would one day, yes."

There was a silence. Then it seemed to register.

"Do you mean now? To you?"

"Well, not now exactly. But of course I mean to me. Do you want me to get down on one knee?"

"Don't be daft."

"So?"

"Oh. OK. Well, yes then."

At last I got a smile out of her. Back in the room, her Filofax soon came out and she wanted to fix a date. I thought it would be a while yet, that we'd have a registry office wedding and a meal with friends. But then, she had a secondary cancer and wanted it as soon as possible. She also hadn't been married before and wanted the whole nine yards of a white wedding and a reception. It would take her about six months to organise properly, she reckoned. I understood both points.

As with her own funeral, she knew how she wanted it. Her maid of honour, Janet, read from the Bible and her friend Claire read a Julia Darling poem (in this case "Two Lighthouses"). Alex, again as she would do at V's funeral, played "The Way You Look Tonight" on the piano.

Afterwards, the reception for our 70 guests was in the village hall, draped and dressed in netting, the colour scheme of the ribbons orange. We feasted on roast beef and Yorkshire pudding. For dessert there was Westfield (not Eton) Mess, named after her school. The tables were all given names of football grounds that meant something to us (Bramall Lane, Wembley, The Wessex Stadium – home of Weymouth FC, where I'd been chairman), and guests found a vintage football programme on their chairs of the team they supported or where they were from. Given our history and the number of games we had been to between us, these were not hard to find.

The beauty of the occasion was that all our friends and family had come from points far and wide and I sensed, even on the day, with me being 55 then, that this could well be the last time we had them all together in one place at the same time.

Vikki looked stunning in the most beautiful traditional white dress and fascinator. She would later say to me that she thought she'd had her hair cut too short, but to me everything about her was gorgeous. She looked utterly radiant. She also made the most charming speech at the reception. Not, of course, without a barb about how long it had taken me finally to see sense.

Mine? I alarmed her at first and she would later say she had wondered where I was going with it. Bear in mind that this was 2010, and we were getting married in an even-numbered year when there was a major football tournament on. This, she said, despite her late father's advice that odd years were therefore best.

"It has been said that it is a triumph of hope over experience," I said. "That despite all the evidence to the contrary, this time it will finally work out successfully and we will live happily ever after."

I could sense some unease in the room, certainly a silence.

"Yet here we are," I continued. "On the verge of a World Cup and still we believe that England can win it."

Alongside me, thankfully, Vikki laughed that throaty, almost dirty laugh of hers and others joined in. The day segued into the night on what was the best 24 hours of my life, ranking alongside the birth of my children. The event was marred only momentarily by my joint best man (with my son Jack) Steve Claridge – formerly of Leicester City and the player-manager I appointed at Weymouth – moaning that this was costing him money as he had had to give up being a radio pundit at a play-off final at Wembley.

Jack played a few numbers on acoustic guitar, including John Martyn's "Couldn't Love You More" and the choir featuring a friend of Vikki's sang a couple of songs.

Our first dance, chosen by Vikki naturally, was the beautiful "Cole's Corner" by the Sheffield guitarist and singer Richard Hawley, once of Pulp. My kids were surprised by my dad-dancing to a soundtrack of tunes that Vikki had assembled on CDs. At the close of the evening, Alex let go into the night sky a couple of lit lanterns, me worrying that they might interfere with nearby Luton Airport.

What was revealed above all by the photos was Vikki beaming all the while. There was that smile that everyone had remarked on and which I had missed, forgotten, those last few months of her life. What made it most special for me, though, was a memory of the two of us alone back home that night not captured by a camera. I can still see Vikki looking me in the eye, her voice giggly with bubbly. I can still hear her saying: "I am SO happy." Cancer felt a long way away. Her chemo of 2007 was behind us. My radiotherapy of 2009 seemed to have worked. Now *that* – to have made someone that happy, someone you loved so much – was a moment to cling on to.

That led to another memory to treasure. The night before the wedding, I was banished to a local hotel while V enjoyed a Prosecco night and a catch-up with half a dozen special friends from her school and university days. When I got to my room and opened my overnight bag, there on the top was a gift of orange cuff links for the morrow and a postcard.

I had always kept it, in a drawer of personal items in a bedside cabinet, and now I went upstairs to find it and sat on the bed, taking in her words. On the front was a quote from a film, *The Wedding Crashers*: "I'm not perfect, but who are we kidding, neither are you." On the back, she had written in black fountain pen: "But I suppose you'll do!!! See you in church. V xxxx."

It was just what I needed to find, to remember, and it would now accompany me everywhere, along with the keyring that was always in my pocket. It was made of copper, which symbolised the eighth anniversary. I had given her a photo frame in the metal with the words "Love and Eight" inscribed. She chose the words "Happy 8th. I Still Do" on the keyring.

The card also sparked in me a desire to find other memorabilia that had meant so much to me, to us.

For much of the time, looking at pictures of good times together simply signalled my sense of loss. That picture of us in Cornwall, for example? She looked great. But then, I won't be going to Cornwall again now... (How could I go without her? It was "our" place... Anyway, I'm ageing now. Running out of time.)

Today, though, I was not feeling what I expected to feel. My sense of loss was still acute, of course, but the wedding album had brought me comfort, reminded me of how fortunate I had been. I decided that pictures of us, rather than pictures of just her, of our past rather than her past, had effected a change. Even if it might be temporary, it was welcome respite.

I decided as a result to hunt for other cards from her, and I'd kept plenty in a shoebox. On top was one prompted by a holiday we had taken three years earlier in Israel and Palestine. At the Garden of Gethsemane, just outside the city walls of Jerusalem, Vikki took a picture of what was claimed to be the oldest olive tree. The tree was supposed to have been there in New Testament times, and had the word Peace spelt out in stones at its base. It was that picture she printed off and glued onto a card that she gave me for Christmas. Inside, she had pasted another picture, of us in the square in Bethlehem and written the words: "copyright OrviceRidley cards". Underneath she wrote:

I

Happy Christmas 2016
and to more fabulous travels in 2017
and beyond.
All possible love
V

All possible love. It made me cry again, but this time they were tears of gratitude.

I looked anew at another card, this one her last birthday card to me from January. (Alex later told me that Vikki had asked her, during her time with us in that January when V was fading, to fetch this card from her desk drawer while I was out.) The difference in the confident handwriting of 2016, if still the journalist's scrawl, was marked. It was spidery but the message remained loving.

"Thanks for everything," she wrote, no doubt referring to the last few months of me trying to make her worsening condition as comfortable as possible. "Oodles of love and hugs. V xxxxx"

It had a drawing of a lighthouse on the front. She loved lighthouses, perhaps because of the hope their light offered. If there was one near wherever we were staying, we had to visit it. I remembered Beachy Head, Portland Bill, and one on Cape Cod in particular. That "Two Lighthouses" poem of Julia Darling's she wanted read at the wedding contained the aspiration that we should live like two lighthouses, "each with her own beam." She wanted us to be in alignment, separate but together.

And then, as I rooted round the house, this time looking for treasure rather than landmines, I found a poem Vikki herself had written. It was from the early days of our relationship.

Thursday Afternoon Poem to I
Loving you (on a good day) is like:
Brazil winning the World Cup every four years.
     And me scoring from your perfect pass.
Sheffield United winning the European Cup (or
     whatever it's called now) every day. And me
     holding the cup aloft. After scoring from your
     perfect pass.

Listening to Van the Man sing Moondance. And It's
    All In The Game. And Warm Love. All rolled
    into one.
A bottle of 18-year-old Macallan. Unopened.
A field full of sunflowers. In Italy.
A Labour victory. Just memorable.
A cup of coffee. Real not instant.
Lippi's La Madonna che adora il Bambino,
    Donatello's David and everything Matisse ever
    painted. All in the same room.
The Wasteland. And the Hollow Men. But with a
    bang not a whimper.
Some Like It Hot. But hotter.
The sun on my back, sand between my toes.
That green dress.
Every single episode of Cheers. Back to back.
The sea at Blakeney Spur. But deeper.

(The "on a good day" bit was scribbled out. I remember when she first showed it to me, after being touched beyond words, asking her why on a good day? She said that she'd inserted it one day when I'd annoyed her but had since crossed it out.)

Once I had finished weeping, that prompted me to look up more of her poetry. And I recalled one that had been published. It came from 2008, written just over a year after her diagnosis and published in a collection of poems by patients, carers and staff of the Royal

Marsden. Its title referred to the month she was told she had cancer.

March Morning
If you had told me a few months earlier
That one Monday morning in March
Just as I was reading the newspapers
I would discover I had cancer
I could only have guessed at my probable reaction.

Scream hysterically
Plan to go to the rest of the 1,000 places I still
    hadn't seen before I die
Scream hysterically.

But I didn't scream
Didn't get on the phone to the travel agent
Didn't scream again.

I just wanted to go to a place I'd seen 1,000 times.
Home.

It was too beautiful and I couldn't stop reading it. Kept it on the coffee table. It chain-linked me to her. I had been the one who picked her up from the hospital after her phone call telling me she had cancer and took her to the place she wanted to go: home. Our home.

And I could still picture her standing on the stage of a lecture theatre at the Marsden on the day of the collection's launch, me beaming with pride as she read out her poem in front of an audience that included the then Poet Laureate, Andrew Motion, who had written a foreword to the book.

I found another remarkable piece of creative writing by her too. A leather-bound notebook in a drawer contained what was clearly the start of a novel. She had spoken often about writing one, based on her time as a student on summer working holidays with a friend in Switzerland and Italy, and using the character of a mysterious old woman on the outskirts of a village where she had taken a temporary job, an old woman who tilled the fields, her breasts exposed to the sun. Vikki wondered what her back story was, whether there had been a tragic love affair. She wanted to call it Night Train to Milan.

Here were the first 10 pages, fluently and elegantly crafted. It was clear it was actually about us. About how we became a couple. Yet more evidence of her love for me. And her talent.

She had also wanted to write a book about her experiences as a female football writer in a man's world, about the funny and the misogynistic. She worried about identifying some of the people in it, though. She liked the title I offered, Saturday Girl (hence how I referred to her in my eulogy at her funeral), and even wrote a synopsis. But she was busy, with a full-time job involving plenty of travelling and a fuller time dealing with the effects of, and treatment for, cancer. I suggested at one point that she stop work and write, that it might be less stressful. We would manage financially, I said. But she would never give up the camaraderie of covering sport for a living. And so she could never finish what she started so achingly beautifully. She just ran out of time.

I also made a point of holding tight the words of those whom I had gone to see or spent hours on the phone with in March, who had said so many touching things about Vikki's love for me. At the time, I had not dwelt on them as I was too much beset by my fears, preoccupied by the questions that had never been answered. I had written them down, though, as is my wont, and now I cherished them:

"You two were made for each other. I said it from the start."

"She loved you so much, I know that."

"Whenever we spoke, she would bring you up straight away."

"She was often frightened she was going to lose you."

"Well, you were the only man she ever wanted. She did tell me that."

"We were all envious of your relationship. We knew it was intense but most people never know that."

I guess I knew this stuff really. But as well as insanity, grief throws up an insecurity that clouds reality. This fear was about my defects and doubts, not hers.

I clung, too, to rituals. Regularly on a Friday while she was alive, I would get the shopping, including two fillet steaks to be cooked in the evening, as well as the long-stemmed roses. That continued, along with lighting a tea light each night in a glass holder that Jacqui Barker, the mother of Darren Barker, the world champion boxer whose autobiography I had written and who came to Vikki's funeral, had so thoughtfully sent me. It bore an inscription quoting my tweet the day V died: "In Loving Memory – My beloved, bright, brilliant Vikki".

I'd ordered a bench in her memory for the cemetery so that I could sit there and read, contemplate and meditate, but it would not be made for a few months yet. And I so bought a folding chair so that I could sit and talk to her of a Friday after I had laid the roses.

And of course photos became vital. I bought frame after frame in which to put the best of those I had printed off for the funeral montages that went in the marquee. Every surface in our bedroom featured one of her or us, every room in the house contained at least two. I wanted her everywhere in our home. They sustained me, often made me smile, sometimes made me cry sweet tears. I talked to them, to her.

Had I turned a corner? Was I over the worse? To be honest, I doubted it. As recovering addicts are prone to feeling – when things are good, they don't believe they will last; when things are bad, they will last for ever. I was simply relieved at some light amid the dark of the pain, however fleeting. I knew the fragility of my state, the depth of the insecurities that could provoke panic attacks from out of the blue. And turn it to black.

Besides, I still had a sense that to feel "better" was to betray her. Plenty of people would tell me: "She wouldn't want you being sad all the time, would want you to move on." But I wasn't so sure. At least, not yet. Just as I'd want, I think she would have appreciated me honouring and acknowledging the depth of what we shared. My sorrow still ran deep and that wasn't going to dissipate this quickly, no matter how many happy snaps I printed off.

For now, going through my checklist of items that meant so much and hearing the voices of those who confirmed her devotion to me, I was content just to acknowledge that memories and memorabilia could be used to fall back on when the demons came calling of a weekend, that they might help keep the vampire from the door.

10

After Tea

· · · · · · · · · · · ·

It was late afternoon on a warm early June day and I'd emerged from an intense two-hour session with Bruce at his consulting room in north London. I didn't want to catch the start of the rush hour, nor go home to an empty house just yet. What to do? Where to go to make sense of what I'd just been through? My mind went back to those times when I had my writing bolthole in Brighton and would sometimes take in the last couple of hours' play of the day in a Sussex match at Hove. And, as it happened, they were playing Middlesex at Lord's...

I tried to park the car in Regent's Park, five minutes' walk from the ground, but Donald Trump was in town and the police had blocked off the area surrounding Winfield House, the American ambassador's residence at the north of the park, where the US President was staying. Instead I found a meter space at the bottom of St John's Wood High Street.

There, waiting for the clock to tick to 4.30 p.m. so that I could put the maximum two hours' fee in to take me to the end of the payment period, I thought of the time Vikki and I went to Winfield House under the previous ambassador, Matthew Barzun, a few years earlier. It was the occasion, believe it or not, of a cricket match in his back garden, which we were told was the second-largest in London, after Buckingham Palace. The match was between the British and American press. Neither of us could quite work out why, but Vikki had received an invitation and we were not questioning the chance.

It was a lovely day, even if the weather was damp. Chairs were set out along a bank overlooking an artificial batting strip on a makeshift pitch. There was southern fried chicken and mini burgers to eat. The US press was being captained by Piers Morgan, not long back from his stint as a chat show host for CNN, and he had recruited his old mate Kevin Pietersen, the England Test batsman. Naturally they easily beat their opponents – mainly TV journalists, captained by Mark Austin. I recall Morgan making a speech afterwards about how he thought that Trump would win the forthcoming election, to the scepticism of most of us. Matthew Barzun – as urbane a man as you might expect, given that he was Barack Obama's pick for the job – said in elegant response that he thought it was better to build bridges rather than walls.

I recall, too, walking arm in arm with Vikki back to the car. She was happy, and relatively healthy thanks to a drug called Palbociclib that the Royal Marsden were trialling. Now I smiled at the memory, just before realising that it was 4.30 p.m.

While I don't recall paying after tea at Hove, here it was a tenner to get in. No matter. It was worth it for a peaceful place to process what had just happened in my session with Bruce. With, of course, some cricket in the background to punctuate the pondering. There was plenty of room to be alone, with perhaps some 500 in the ground, dotted about in the areas that were open. I plumped for the Compton Stand, as near to straight on with the wicket as possible without being too near to the buffs and their chatter.

Sussex were well on top. Having bowled out Middlesex on day one for 138, they were 412 for seven at tea on this, the second day. Ben Brown had made a century and Stiaan van Zyl was unbeaten on 142. This was painful to watch for any Middlesex follower who was used to the county being one of the powerhouses of domestic cricket, and county champions just two years earlier, but now floundering in Division Two.

My hour with Bruce had been painful too, but necessary, exposing the rawness of my nerves but throwing light on why I had been suffering debilitating anxiety attacks. As soon as he opened the door, I burst into tears. He hugged me and I moved into his office. I couldn't take the seat opposite him today, though. There was a sofa in the corner. I had been left exhausted by my fitful sleeping pattern and just collapsed onto it, sobbing loudly.

Bruce had rescued me from emotional crises many times down the years. Wise and wizened, he began life as an addiction counsellor working in various treatment centres. After setting up on his own in south London, he developed a reputation as something of a maverick, guru or shaman, to whom seekers of freedom from, or at least understanding of, the lingering issues that the now clean and sober were experiencing. He kept himself under the media radar despite many well-known people beating a path to his door.

He was no grief counsellor, though he had much experience of grief, but had grown to believe that various traumas we undergo in earlier years can become triggered all over again by events in our lives and come back to haunt us. By revisiting the traumas, grasping what lay beneath them and acknowledging our shame and fear, we could at least learn to cope with the damaging effects of their reappearances.

I was sceptical when he introduced me to the concept of trauma being past events, which could even be from way back into our childhood, that left scars. It could be anything from abuse to neglect, even unconscious neglect, which can produce lasting emotional damage, and would have different resonances for different people. It often resurfaced, dragging us down and back. It would be too much to say that we can heal completely from it. To believe so was probably to have unrealistic expectations. But we could learn to cope and not let the trauma stop us from living fully and achieving. As he used to say to me: "Ian, you are always going to walk with a limp. But you will walk."

At first, I found all this hard to take in. Nothing really bad had happened to me, I said. Not compared to others. I'd had a good, lucky life. Trauma was for those subjected to terrible events – servicemen and women, or those in accidents, for example. Yet I came to see how life was an echo chamber for us all, and how my fears and anxieties could be provoked anew by deep-seated memories of what had unnerved and undermined me in the past. And long and intense sessions with Bruce had uncovered what the voices of doubt and self-sabotage were.

Today was certainly long and intense and part of his work with me that was saving my life – and not just in having persuaded me to accept the cancer treatment. He was that guy you see in movies who says the right things to some desperate soul likely to do something silly.

"I get the sadness," I said to Bruce when I could speak. "I just didn't expect this madness."

I told him how I'd worked consciously on recalling good memories of Vikki and me, and how it had worked for a while. But always the fear returned. I had finally got around to starting C.S. Lewis's touchstone book, *A Grief Observed*, which a thoughtful friend had recommended back in March, and been grabbed by its opening line: "No one ever told me that grief felt so much like fear."

And still there were those nervy Saturday nights, with my mind taking me to dark places and my imagination running riot. Of obsessions, questions I had never asked and thus never had answers to. What were the secrets she kept? Were there any indeed? What were the diaries *not* saying?

Pretty soon, I realised – or was gently led to realise – that this was not about Vikki, what she may or may not have done. She was her own person, after all. Her life before she met me was none of my business. Nor indeed, in many ways, was her life when she was apart from me. We all have choices in life. Whether or not to stay and live with people, to make the best of those lives. And I chose to believe that we were loyal to each other, there being no evidence to the contrary. The evidence of her gestures towards me and the testimony of her friends was that she loved me truly, madly and deeply, as I did her. Ian, for goodness sake, have a word with yourself. She did nothing wrong.

My head told me all that. But my darkness, the triggers for my trauma, troubled me at a visceral level. In my raw and vulnerable state, this was about me and my personal characteristics as a recovering alcoholic who had drunk on fear and shame in times past, who in his teenage angst had agonised over losing girlfriends to, as I perceived it, more handsome and stronger blokes, who had also felt a trauma of being abandoned by key women at impressionable moments in his life.

Bruce took me through my reactions to the diaries and the photos to show where it had all come from. It inevitably involved returning to moments in childhood and adolescence, examining my family of origin. This, I came to see, was about people close to me not being available to me, for whatever reason, and my desperate need to reconnect with them. My panic was about the insecurity, embedded in me many years ago, of a key relationship in my life having been severed. And that had resurfaced in my relationship with Vikki. Now it had been severed for good. There had been times when we were apart but we had always known deep down that we would reconnect, that the other would eventually be available again. Now, for the first time, this was not going to happen. Could not.

Between noisy sobs, I told Bruce that what I wanted was just to see V again. Just once more. To talk it all through, to tie up loose ends. To tell her how I really felt, to hear answers to old questions. Above all, I wanted to start again, for us to have all the knowledge of ourselves of the past 20 years and to know that we would be OK, that it would be OK, and we could stop worrying and just enjoy each other's company.

But of course, I realised, life cannot ever be like that, I said to Bruce as I and my session unravelled. The trick is making the most of it while you have it. So simple to say, so hard to live. Daily events can intrude. Only the wisest – and I didn't feel that was me in my current fog – actually implement the now, rather than believe that we'll savour it all at some nebulous future date once we've managed this phase of our life. There's no escaping, though, that even the wisest will suffer from regrets and what ifs. That is the human condition.

I just fucking wish though, I added, that there was a rewind button. The person who invents that will end up richer than Bill Gates. Bruce smiled.

I had been seeing him weekly, and would continue to do so, but this day felt significant. The obsession and insanity of my grief was raw, our conversation wide-ranging. It all poured out in a torrent. I told him how nothing mattered, not the football matches on in the background these days as I pottered restlessly around the house. I couldn't watch drama series or other TV programmes I had watched with Vikki. I couldn't even watch films that contained any kind of romance or sexual encounter. They just reminded me of what I had lost, was missing. I couldn't bear the thought of going to the cinema without her.

I was sorry, I told him, that we hadn't taken more holidays together, that we had not hugged each other enough, sat together on the sofa watching TV instead of in separate chairs. Above all, I was sorry that we had never had a child together. There just never seemed to be an opportune time, and by the time we were finally settled, Vikki was 42 and I was 50. We both had demanding jobs that preoccupied us. Time had slipped through my, our, fingers.

I was exhausted by all of this. Depressed even. My appetite had deserted me. The new cancer drug I was on only added to my debilitation. I understood, I added, why the bereaved often also die within a couple of years of the death of their partner, as my father had.

Usually, Bruce would listen for 20 minutes to half an hour, making notes that he would provide me with at the end of the session, then summarise before offering his thoughts.

He reminded me that around 15 years earlier, at Vikki's request, he had seen her for half a dozen sessions on her own, then us together. Both of us, he said, suffered from fear of abandonment due to trauma – events, neglects and omissions – during formative years. As a result, we both worried that the life – the partner – we had worked so hard for, would be somehow snatched away from us.

It was why, he suggested, we sometimes didn't tell each other everything, that we kept small secrets from each other, as we were concerned that the other might leave. He could not tell me, he said, what passed between him and Vikki in their sessions, but those small secrets, like mine, were about the trivial, about maybe financial resentments or time not spent together. The human, the everyday. It was a fear of intimacy – less physically, more emotionally – caused by the fear of abandonment from key developmental periods in early life. My jealousies, he said, had sent me "barking up the wrong tree," adding: "Trust me, I have a lot of miles on the clock when it comes to intuition." He had told her, as he told me now, that as well as all the traditional comforts our partners offer, they are sometimes also there, uncomfortably, to provide opportunities to grow.

Abandonment suggests a willing act. That somebody has done something deliberately. But Vikki, to my intense sadness and sympathy, had had no control about leaving me. She had died. My head knew that but my psyche didn't. I had been abandoned and it was triggering the darkest time of my life. I was pining for the woman who had mirrored me, made me.

What I called insanity, Bruce described as the swamp of panic. It was that overlapping place in a Venn diagram of where grief and trauma met.

Insanity
(aka: the swamp of panic)

Our problem, he said – and what had frustrated him – was that our separate traumas and insecurities too often clouded our love for each other. We found something in each other that created deep and powerful emotions, as friends had noted. Sometimes for good, when we were the luckiest couple ever, and sometimes bad.

I offered Bruce a football analogy that made him smile. When we were on form, I said, we could beat Manchester City. We were amazing together, made for each other. When work, life, our issues intervened and we rubbed each other up the wrong way, we could go out of the cup to a Non-League team.

Bruce was always a counter-intuitive man, one who saw life from a different angle, and that was why I loved and trusted him. He would generously offer you his own vulnerabilities and scars that comprised his experience and wisdom. Somebody once called him a one-eyed man leading us blind people.

I had many lovely, well-meaning friends who offered help but not always the most fitting advice. Some told me to ignore all that obsessional stuff about the past, about regrets of what was said and done, not said and done. Just get over it. Let it go. Others told me to hang in there. Bruce urged me to revisit and embrace it, if not physically by going back into the diaries and photos that had remained untouched since March. He told me that, by acknowledging my trauma, familiarity with it would diminish its power over me. In sporting terms, if you're going to overcome the opposition, you need to read the scouting report.

He advised me then to write down the testimony of her friends about her devotion to me and read it regularly, hold on to those memories and mementos that had sustained me recently when the going got tough: the cards from the wedding, Jerusalem, my last birthday. The wedding anniversary keyring, the selfie of us on holiday with her head on my shoulder in a gesture of love. How, on the day she was told her cancer was closing in on her, she'd told me that I'd been the love of her life. These, he said, would be counterpoints to the doubts and regrets and would help me create a narrative that confirmed her love for me and the validity of our life together.

Now, you can't really think about ideas as essential and deep as all of that at a football match, especially with somebody berating the ref in your ear. In fact, the game probably exists to get away from it all. But at county cricket, with its less frenetic unfolding, a person could connect with what really mattered. That day, a game of complex nuances felt just right to sit with life's complex nuances.

I watched Van Zyl's quest for a double hundred that ended at 173, Sussex soon after declaring at 481 for nine. (Once-mighty Middlesex, who would finish eighth of 10 at season's end, would be bowled out for 293 in their second innings over the next two rain-affected days and lose by an innings and 50 runs.) At the close, I departed with the other solitary souls and suddenly felt hungry. This would be far from the end of my grief. Far from the end of the beginning of my grief. Not even the beginning of the end. In fact, I was sure it would never end. But it had been a while since I felt properly hungry. That had to say something.

Addicts and alcoholics never quit their drug of choice on the basis of self-knowledge, so the perceived wisdom goes, and I had seen plenty of truth in that down the years. After all, they often know they are damaging and defeating themselves and others but they are in the grip of an illness and cannot stop without some kind of rock-bottom experience and a desire for the madness to stop. And so I knew that the insight into my trauma would not stop the pain of living now without Vikki, and all the feelings that was stirring in me. It felt, though, like a shift, a staging post in the process of somehow learning to find meaning to living again. The pain, I knew, would return along with all the fears prompted by the past, present and future, and I would come to know what those who had been through this meant by the waves of grief.

But as I drove home from Lord's ready to stomach a meal, I felt a lightness – or perhaps more accurately, less of a heaviness – a pleasant weariness, at the relief of knowing what was going on with me, of there being reasons underlying how I was feeling beyond the grief, and having some measure of defence against what I was dealing with whenever it returned.

11

State of Grace

· · · · · · · · · · · · · · · · · ·

I'd wanted to go and see the return fixture between Nottinghamshire and Hampshire at Welbeck Cricket Club as the location had a meaning for Vikki. Her mother, Jean, was from nearby Shirebrook, her maiden name French (as in Bruce, the Warsop-born Notts wicket-keeper to whom she was related in some way that I never quite grasped when V told me). However, my plans were scuppered by another staple of an English summer: three days of rain.

It was now June and the Championship was starting to fall between the cracks of cricket's summer. After the Welbeck wash-out, I had to wait a week to find a convenient match that also had a resonance, Leicestershire v Gloucestershire at Grace Road, a ground named not after W.G. but a local property developer.

We'd been to Leicester often down the years, notably to see Alex during her time at De Montfort University in the same city where Vikki had gone to university, and to this ground for a T20 match. And of course to cover football in this sporting-daft town, home to the Premier League champions of 2016 and top Rugby Union team, the Tigers. In fact, I always thought Leicester resembled – not in looks, admittedly – Boston, Massachusetts as a provincial, smaller city with its variety of teams who competed at the top level of their sports.

There was, too, a link with the opposition. Vikki's last job in the provinces before coming to Fleet Street was on the *Western Daily Press* in Bristol, where she had risen to news editor. She once showed me a wonderful set of photos of her in her mid-twenties modelling an evening dress for a photo shoot for the paper. The model hadn't turned up for a feature for the fashion pages and Vikki, as one the few females in the office, was asked if she'd do it. She did, just to see the look on people's faces, and was mighty proud of her first and only modelling shoot. So should she have been.

Today, the third of the match, got off to an inauspicious start when I turned up at the Bennett End of the cricket ground. I had seen that Leicestershire were charging £10 for parking for the day and drove up to the car park entrance. There, however, I was told that I could only come in if I had pre-booked a space.

"But it's empty," I replied.

"Yes," replied one of the two gatekeepers. "But them's the rules." At this point, he turned to his mate. "I've told them, 'aven't I?" he said. His mate nodded. Then he turned to me. "I said, I've told the powers that be that we should be letting people in without having booked but they've not listened."

Parking was free in the street, he pointed out helpfully, and indeed I parked 20 yards away and saved myself a tenner. I came back and paid my £12 match admission to the same gatekeepers. It seemed ridiculously cheap. With parking, they could have had thirty quid out of me that day without me complaining.

It was a muggy morning. The sort of weather to give you a headache. I had plenty of choice of seat – in fact, I had a choice of row to myself. There were about 60 people in the ground at start of play, a figure that would rise to around 100 by lunchtime. They were easy to count.

The ground itself was a functional, unlovely place but had its charms. The pavilion was plain, stands and buildings had been erected down the years as and when the county had the wherewithal. Here at the Bennett End, there were now offices and indoor nets. At least it had its own character. Cricket still had grounds rather than just stadia. Too many football clubs had rebuilt their homes to look just like any other.

Leicestershire were a slightly better side these days (though they would finish bottom of Division Two with just one win) than earlier in the decade, when they went almost three seasons without winning a four-day game – 993 days and 37 games, in fact. On the first two days of this match, they had amassed 487 in their first innings, then reduced Gloucestershire to 41 for three in the gloaming of the previous evening.

"Batted a long time yesterday," said Man One to Man Two sitting a row in front five yards to the side of me.

"Too long to my mind," said Man Two.

Such concerns seemed academic, though, as Leicestershire claimed two more wickets before lunch, leaving Gloucestershire wobbling at 131 for five. Leicestershire must even have been entertaining the prospect of enforcing the follow-on, 150 runs behind the opposition's total being the margin in county cricket (200 in Tests). Even so, it wasn't good enough, apparently.

"Thought we might have done better this morning in these conditions," said Man One. Man Two nodded. Soon they were applauding a half-century by the Bristolian Chris Dent. I have always liked that about cricket: the fair-minded applause for an opponent's achievements.

"We never get him out," said Man Two. I liked that too. These were diehards. People who knew their cricket and cricketers, even the other team's. And people who settled into a game in which little was happening by seeking conversational digression, as cricket was wont to do.

"You don't need that at this age," sympathised Man One as they swopped ailments.

Soon, a third man arrived to join in such fun (which included lamenting that Leicestershire were operating without a fielder in the third man position) and the talk turned to how cold it had been the previous evening.

Really? I thought. I didn't remember that. Then came the reason for his observation: a retelling of a dad joke he had clearly just heard.

"I told the wife to get her coat and she asked me if we were going out," he said. "'No,' I said, 'I'm not turning the heating on.'"

I caught myself smiling, then feeling guilty. Damn. I had nearly made it through a two-hour session of cricket without worrying either about my cancer or the prospect of life now meaning loneliness. The mention of a wife had sent me back into my reality, however. And feeling that a slither of enjoyment was wrong when Vikki could not enjoy anything.

Her name coming into my head – actually it was always there, just more dormant at some times than others – prompted another memory of being with her in this city more than 20 years earlier. I had just ghostwritten a book for the co-best man at our wedding, Steve Claridge, who was playing for Leicester at the time, and we had come to a local bookshop to do a signing.

(One man, I recall, asked Steve to sign a photo of his cat, whom he had named Claridge. "From one Claridge to another," wrote Steve.) Vikki asked if she might borrow my car to visit an old friend in Leicester for an hour. Of course, I said. Some hours later, I noticed a dent in the back of it. "Must have been someone in the car park bumping into it," she said. Only years later did she admit she had reversed into a post. The memory amused me but also saddened. I would happily take her putting dents in my car now.

Clearly I was never going to escape grief at cricket, especially with the game's potential for brooding time, but one of its manifold attractions was its ability to distract. At home, my fermenting feelings followed me round the house. Here, I could get up and wander, at least. Lunch was approaching. Time for a sandwich hunt at the Pavilion End.

I found what I was looking for in The Meet cafe. Only in the East Midlands, it seems, can you get cheese rolls with raw onion. I used to have them every even day (pie and mushy peas with gravy and mint sauce on odd days) at lunchtimes in my first job in sports journalism, on the *Worksop Guardian*, with a nice – a word made for tea – hot, strong cup of char to wash it down.

At most county cricket venues, I was discovering, there was an area set aside for the sale of second-hand sports books. And here, right next to the cafe, they were £3 for hardbacks or £1 for paperbacks, with an "honesty" tray for the money. All hail most county cricket venues.

With its big windows, even if the view was side on, the cafe seemed like a good place to camp for the after-noon. Well, it saved the walk back for tea and cake (home-made, the sign insisted) in a couple of hours. And the snatches of overheard conversation were promising.

"You coming to the Twenty-Twenties?" said one slightly less grumpy old man to another grumpy old man. The T20 tournament was just a couple of weeks away.

"No, they're night games," came the reply.

"But that's when most people want to come to watch."

"I don't care. I'm not coming."

There was a pause.

"According to the *Express*, it's going to rain a lot over the next month."

"Serves them right. That's all I can say."

It wasn't clear whether the "them" were T20 spectators or the *Daily Express*, but clearly it was being so cheerful that kept him going. I gave thanks that while I was sad, probably even going in and out of depressions, I was not as curmudgeonly as that, although V would have said that I had my moments. And while I may not have loved T20, I didn't want others to suffer because of that. Sometimes you have to be grateful to others not for the inspiration they offer, but for the realisation that your world view is not as gloomy as perhaps you thought it was.

My mind wandered. In the early days after Vikki's death – and probably these were still early days – I had the sense that so many who are bereaved talk of: that they cannot understand how and why people are still carrying on going about their business as if nothing had happened. I didn't resent them, I was just genuinely baffled. My world had collapsed and I was walking through their world dazed but they weren't reacting. How could this be? At times I simply wanted to stop someone and say: "My wife has just died, you know." I think Vikki must have felt that too at the death of her father back in 1996. (She and her mother Jean had had inscribed on Fred's headstone: "He was our North, South, East and West," from the W.H. Auden poem "Stop All The Clocks".) For the bereaved, there is no control over others and little to be done except to get over it and oneself and pretty quickly. People couldn't possibly know or be expected to care like I did as her husband, lover, soulmate and carer, and I had to understand that the world, their world, would keep turning. For them, nothing *had* happened.

I recalled one recent Friday when I called in at a sandwich bar while carrying the flowers I had bought that day for Vikki's grave. The young woman behind the counter remarked how pretty the flowers were.

"They for anyone special?" she asked.

"My wife," I replied.

"That's nice," she said. "A special occasion?"

I felt I was on the spot. I should have just smiled, maybe told a white lie, said something about an anniversary. Instead, I just blurted it out.

"They're for her grave."

She looked embarrassed. "So sorry to hear that."

I felt bad for her. But then, I always wanted to speak about Vikki at every possible opportunity. I wanted to keep her memory alive, for me as much as for others. She was just always on my mind. There was no escape. Nor did I want any. No wonder I was so exhausted – sometimes without being able to sleep – as I lay in bed at nights reviewing the day, every move and every conversation. On days when I made any move or had conversations.

Now, out in the middle, Dent and the Zimbabwean Ryan Higgins were rebuilding the Gloucestershire innings with some comfort, revealing their five wickets to fall thus far to be the result of tired shots after almost two days of fielding rather than any spite in the clearly placid wicket. At tea (I went for the banana cake; a little dry), both were still unbeaten and the game was meandering.

As the conversation had been. We were in the midst of the various rounds of the Conservative Party leadership contest. "Don't care much for any of them," said the less grumpy old man. Of more concern was the recent announcement by the BBC – who had been placed in a difficult position by a government refusing to increase the licence fee by what the Beeb felt was necessary – that free licences for the over-75s were to be scrapped.

"Well, I'll not watch telly then," said the other grumpy old man.

"It's only £3 a week."

"I don't care if it's 3p or £3. It's the principle of it."

I decided on a walk back to the other end to watch the evening session, to be near the car, ready for a swift getaway. Not that there would be a sudden rush of cars leaving. It was more that the Leicester rush hour, I knew from some previous experience, and the route back to the M1 could get a little busy. At least, from this angle, I could avoid the Narborough Road, which always seemed to be chocka.

On Dent and Higgins batted. And on. Past 300. Scanning the ground, I thought back to this morning and paying my measly £12, along with the hundred or so others. There was simply no way that the revenue we were contributing was covering the salaries of the players out there and sitting on the dressing-room balcony, let alone the coaching staff. The finances of county cricket, like lower League and Non-League football, often made little sense to me but here particularly you wondered how the club survived. The answer had to be the 20-over form of the game. The beleaguered Leicestershire finance director was probably ticking off the days on the office calendar, unlike the grumpy old man.

I was suddenly grateful that there were people in what was no doubt an under-pressure commercial department working to bring in the funds to keep the extended form of the game going for such as me, enabling it to retain its integrity or even just survive. To many, it may seem quaint, an anachronism, but – as with those who promote the Cornish language or are still prepared to look daft while Morris dancing – I was glad that, despite the multitude of modern sporting diversions, its gentle competitiveness remained part of the fabric of English life and culture during this summer of my greatest need.

On Dent and Higgins batted. And on. Past 400. I had plenty of time to finish a crossword. To check Twitter. And it was noticeable and surprising that, while youngsters get criticism for being on their phones all the time, there were plenty of middle-aged, even old, men texting or trying to suppress their ringtones.

My day was all going a bit too well. It was all a bit too quiet. I couldn't have that. And so, as if getting in my retaliation first, as if seeking to try and control the pain rather than be taken by surprise by it, I began to feel those waves of grief people describe. And wave is an apt word. It washes over you, leaves you drenched in sadness.

On Dent and Higgins batted. And on. But wait, here comes a gap between the waves. At 449, Dent fell for 176. The 318 they had put on for the sixth wicket was a Gloucestershire record. (Forgive me, cricket loves a statistic and it is easy to get seduced by the order they embody). Being agitated now, it felt like a good time to make an escape, change my location, steal a march on the Leicester ring road. Later, I would hear that Gloucestershire had closed on 503 for six, with Higgins 196 not out. There would surely be little to no chance of a result the following day with two such mammoth first-innings totals, and my appetite for returning was small.

So it would prove. Higgins was out one short of his double century as Gloucestershire reached 571 all out. After that, both Leicestershire openers, Hasan Azad and Paul Horton, made unbeaten centuries – Azad thus scoring a ton in both innings – before both captains shook hands on a tame draw.

There we had it: some 1,250 runs in four days all for nothing, apart from bonus points. Those for whom the game made little sense would have had fodder for their bemusement at the futility of it all. But such was the appeal of cricket, the honour of a draw after honest toil by bowlers on an unhelpful pitch on which batsmen with a glint in their eyes had taken their chances to boost averages.

I'd found some respite for eight hours or so, but now edginess accompanied me down the M1. I was still a repository of regrets, at times, about the past and fear of a future alone. A prisoner of my own insecurities, which clashed with my grieving. I could be comfortable in my own company at times – fleeting times – but more often anxious that I could fall ill, or just fall, and no one would be on hand any more to help. Add my cancer having returned into this volatile mix, and it could feel all-consuming.

· 12 ·

I Found a Picture of You

I suppose I should have been grateful – seen it as a sign that I was beginning to return to what I remember my parents calling "the land of the living" on a Sunday morning after one of their major Saturday nights out – that I was starting to worry about my own health. I'd been to the dentist for the first time in a couple of years, due to a nagging toothache, and was also now a few months into the cancer treatment, the new tablets having had the desired effect and brought down my PSA level.

Vikki would have been pleased that I had followed her example and taken whatever the Marsden recommended. I thought about how she took everything on offer to her, every drug, every treatment and clung to life for as long as she could. It was precious to her, to be drunk in long gulps. I was never as outgoing as her, but part of my duty now, as I saw it, was honouring her character and resilience, and mirroring her trust in the Marsden's skills.

I spent a lot of time asking myself in any situation, at any time of day: what would Vikki do? What would she say? As C.S. Lewis wrote: "Her absence was like the sky, spread over everything."

(His book *A Grief Observed* – about the loss of his wife, the American poet Joy Davidman, to cancer and which was the basis for the film *Shadowlands* – had become essential reading for me. It was perfect for the stage of my grief I had reached, some five months after Vikki's passing. It was just 60 pages long and I could read it five pages at a time and absorb it, marvelling at its perceptiveness.)

And I did plenty for her, too, around the house, things that I felt she would have wanted done had she lived. I bought a new fridge, had a new boiler installed. The windows of the house, neglected these past couple of years, were repaired and repainted. She would have approved, and would have too of our friend Moira potting some beautiful, colourful flowers for the front of our house. I was coming to love flowers, and began buying them to place all around the house, including orange roses for our bedroom.

I'd had so long worrying about Vikki's health that I'd put mine on the back burner. I'd done all the regular blood tests and clinic appointments for the results, and could live with the side effects of my drugs – fatigue, hot flushes, joint ache – because they simply didn't compare with what V was going through. Now, having made a decision to keep living, I worried about every little ache and pain. My scan in April had also shown up a little shadow in the ribcage that had the doctor wondering what it was – whether I'd had a fall in the previous months, and indeed I did take a tumble in the hotel in Southwold in January when trying to lift Vikki – and it made me fret that my cancer had spread yet further. One day, after feeling my back hurting when taking a shower, I rang the Marsden and described my symptoms. They thought it nothing sinister, and to see if it persisted until my next check-up in a month or so.

The anxiety had first hit me at Leicester that cricket day and it was probably no more than the fact that my seat was uncomfortable, the pain the result of this slouchy figure, his posture shockingly bad due to a lifetime of writing (like Vikki, though her shoulders were not as round as mine) and sitting in one place for more than an hour. I reminded myself of what I used to tell V whenever she would grow sensitive about aches and colds. "Not everything is about cancer, you know." I always was terrible at listening to myself.

It was also probably much to do with the fact I needed something else to worry about, somewhere to divert my obsessional thinking and the panics when they returned – less often, I had to admit, but still intense when they did. I couldn't stop myself listening in bed one night in the dark to a programme on Radio 4 in the Digital Human series entitled *Obsession*, and hearing people who had suffered from "retroactive jealousy" and didn't understand their compulsive need for answers, what somebody called a "quest for certainty". I was tempted to turn the radio off as this was like rubber-necking an accident involving myself. But gradually, the programme dragged me in, as I identified only too closely with the need to "search to reduce suffering". That was what Joan Didion had also experienced. I'm glad I stuck with it. There came a conclusion that I was meant to hear.

Those who survived their obsession seemed to suggest that no amount of searching for evidence from the past to try and find answers we think we need was going to satisfy my curiosity. As one of the people being interviewed said: "I was the one with the problem here. I was not going to research my way out of this problem." This really wasn't about Vikki or anything to do with her. This was about acceptance that I was not in control of a process, nor the timing of how long it might last, and that I needed to find a way to let go. It was about self-worth and fear, about issues of insecurity. Not about answers. Easier said than done, of course, but it was another brick in the wall of my understanding.

I began to understand, too, that all of this quagmire of pain was actually getting in the way of my proper grieving process. That because I didn't want to feel Vikki's loss so acutely, and the brutality of loneliness, I stayed stuck in my own morass.

And how I missed her. I missed her humanity. She was the one who helped me connect with other people. She was a social animal who loved the theatre, cinema, art galleries, holidays. Who loved the company of other people. I was the hermit she – thankfully – forced to interact with other people. My instinct now, self-destructively, was to hide away a lot of the time without her and suppress the humanity she brought out in me, not risk interacting with people and getting hurt, so bound up in my own emptiness was I.

Naturally, left to my own devices, I could feel a terrible sadness at her death and a fear of my own. It just didn't seem right that she had gone at the age of 56 while I was still alive. I couldn't avoid the regular feeling that I was the one who really should have gone first, such was her vivacity and my more internalised life. Also in my aloneness, I could experience extreme emotions within a few minutes of each other. There would be gloom at the gaping hole in my life but not far behind could come a huge gratitude for her love and the aliveness she had shared with me.

I had to be careful about my anger surfacing too. One day, just taking in the view at my favourite place in London, Primrose Hill, I saw a woman on her phone paying no attention as her three dogs took dumps in the grass. I was fuming and shouted across to tell her so, about how kids played on this patch of ground. She was at least apologetic but it took her a while to end her call before getting out some plastic bags and looking for the offending piles. Later, I told a friend about how annoyed I had been when I could have been less aggressive. "Good to see we're getting the old Ian back," he said with a smile.

I recall the arrival of another Saturday this midsummer. I just didn't want to be alone all day with myself and the tension that always built up come weekend evenings. I would often get butterflies in my stomach as a prelude to the panic. Indeed, I would be in such a funk that I couldn't concentrate even on simple tasks like emptying the rubbish bin. If I did manage to start them, I would get sidetracked and begin others when halfway through, so that the black bag was left in a hallway. Similarly, I could not remember what I'd done yesterday. This wasn't just the ageing process, or the blokeishness that used to mean I could remember the 1967 FA Cup winners (Spurs) but not something that Vikki had asked me to do that morning. This was the preoccupation of pain.

A passage in *A Grief Observed* that I had marked – one of many passages now noted by highlighter pen – told of my state that first surfaced in March and which would return to haunt me at intervals:

Tonight all the hells of young grief have opened again; the mad words, the bitter resentment, the fluttering in the stomach, the nightmare unreality, the wallowed-in tears. For in grief, nothing "stays put". One keeps on emerging from a phase, but it always recurs. Round and round. Everything repeats. Am I going in circles, or dare I hope I am on a spiral?

But if a spiral, am I going up or down it?

There's a belief among many people trying to recover
from addictive illnesses that when such moments strike,
you should "sit with the feelings", acknowledge and own
them rather than run away from them. By facing them,
their power lessens for the next time. I was on first-name
terms with my feelings, though; knew them intimately. It
occurred to me that I should probably be spending *less*
time sitting with my feelings. So, one Saturday morning,
I decided to finish something that I'd started.

The summer before she died, Vikki had been determined to have a new kitchen installed. We'd lived on
salads made in an adjacent room for a month while
it was done. Chosen by her, the kitchen was typically
tasteful but to me now, without her colour around it,
it just felt bland and antiseptic. And so I went back to
the photos of us on my phone and hers. I found those
of us enjoying meals or afternoon tea out together – in
Italy, Jerusalem, Bruges, at Le Manoir in Oxfordshire
for her birthday, at Buckingham Palace that year ago
now. Ah, there was that picnic in the Cotswolds when
she hired a vintage Mercedes sports car as a birthday
present for me for the most perfect couple of days. It
meant yet another trip back to print some off in Boots,
where they must have been having suspicions about me,
and then finding a large frame to accommodate them
all. The result was a montage of memories to go on a
wall that would make me smile every morning when I
walked into the kitchen, bleary-eyed and scratchy from

lack of sleep, to make the first cup of tea for the day. As I put the photos together, I couldn't help recalling a couple of lines from a Pretenders song, "Back on the Chain Gang", about finding a picture of a loved one, and those being the happiest days of my life. I put a title on the montage: Eat, Drink, Love.

Now it was done and I couldn't sit here all day admiring my handiwork. I looked for a cricket match to go to. There was none. The World Cup was in full swing and there was no county cricket scheduled. It felt to me like the authorities had missed a trick. They clearly wanted people to focus on the tournament but for those whose interest had been piqued by the competition, there should have been something more accessible.

I watched a World Cup match on TV for a while but sport on television these days was more often just a backdrop to me as I pottered around the house. In my edgy state, I grew restless after half an hour of just sitting and watching. It was a sunny day too. And so I wandered over to my local village playing field, where cricket of a sort was being played. I could walk the boundary rope. Sit untroubled on a bench.

The penchant for shouting – of wicketkeepers loudly acknowledging every reasonable ball or decent piece of fielding as if those who had achieved them might grow downcast if not praised highly enough – had filtered down to this level too, as did Premier League antics to playground football matches. Still, it was pleasant

enough sitting, out of the house, hearing the crack of
leather on cross-batted willow in between the shouting.

On my walk over to the cricket field, I had bumped
into vicar Tom, who was out on a bike ride. He told me
that he would join me soon. I had been watching the
game, with all its missed full tosses, for about half an
hour when he arrived. I don't think he was part of the
suicide-watch rota of Vikki's lovely friends in the village
but clearly he remained concerned for me, wanted to help.

Having been working on the photo montage that
morning, I told Tom about it, about trying to focus on the
items that prompted happy memories of our life together
in my attempt to get out from under the yoke of loss.
He asked me how I was. Mixed, I told him. It came and
went. Not quite as bad as March, I said, when he'd come
round to see me in my anxiety. Then, as I took stock
here in the sunshine rather than behind closed doors, I
thought about another sentence in C.S. Lewis, about the
guilt of feeling better. (I looked it up when I got home.
It read: "There's no denying that in some sense I 'feel
better', and with that at once comes a sort of shame and
a feeling that one is under a sort of obligation to cherish
and foment and prolong one's unhappiness.")

Tom knew *A Grief Observed* and we discussed it, particularly this idea of feeling guilty about any "improve-
ment" in my condition, as if it was disloyal to V. But he
was with Lewis: that to continue the depth of mourning intensely and indefinitely is to block the memory of

shared joys. "Passionate grief," wrote Lewis, "does not link us with the dead but cuts us off from them." In this way, Tom pointed out, to wallow in death is to deny the celebration of life. Lewis found himself equally surprised by this realisation. "Why has no one told me these things? How easily I might have misjudged another man in the same situation? I might have said, 'He's got over it. He's forgotten his wife,' when the truth was, 'He remembers her better *because* he has partly got over it.'"

As we discussed the beautifully expressed sense that Lewis made, I had to admit that while I had glimmers of the sort of awareness and insight that he had reached, the ideas remained mostly aspirations rather than my reality. That was OK, I had to tell myself; as people such as Tom and Bruce were telling me, and Lewis also noted, this was a process not a permanent state. I was still taking small steps. As compiling the photo montage had also showed, remembering the good times allayed the grief for a short time. That was OK too. It wasn't that I was avoiding it, it was just that my body and soul were preparing themselves naturally to cope physically, mentally and emotionally with the next passage of grieving.

I thanked Tom for his company and wisdom. I'd had enough of wickets tumbling for few runs on the village field and so I made my way home. There the photos showed none of the conflict that beset us on occasion – as was inevitable when both were so passionate and alike – to obscure the love. But they revealed how short a period three to seven years was, which was my tentative cancer prognosis. Some of the moments frozen in time seemed only yesterday, and I could remember the circumstances around them: the boat ride to the restaurant in Camogli in Italy where we loved to holiday, the walk up the hill. The resilience of her walking to Claridge's hotel from the car for afternoon tea on her birthday just three months before she died. That trip to Bruges to celebrate the 10th anniversary since her diagnosis, a decade of survival.

Some friends were suggesting that I might now benefit from a summer holiday, and I did think about going back to Camogli for a week, about returning to the place where we were often happiest, to buy the staff, who came to recognise us when we arrived, a drink to toast my lost love. To walk the ground we had trodden together this time last year a few months before cancer's ravages became so demanding.

I quickly abandoned any notions that I would pay some kind of romantic homage to Vikki, however. It would just be a lonely blubfest, a panicky prison of memories – happy ones, yes, but a reminder that I would no longer have her to share such moments with. Besides, I still couldn't be away from the house and her sensed presence in it for more than a couple of nights.

Perhaps, though, there was a place closer to home I could go for a short break, one that held memories not quite so overwhelming and which involved doing something I was coming to look forward to and cherish.

· 13 ·

Scarbados

In the autumn of 2007, when Vikki was still undergoing her first chemotherapy, we had to cancel a week in North Yorkshire at a quiet hotel near Whitby. They allowed us to defer the booking until the following year. And so, after she had covered the Olympic Games in Beijing and with her now in remission, we took the chance for a bit of rest and relaxation.

She was particularly keen to take me to Scarborough for a day, wanting to revisit and show me all the haunts she remembered fondly from her childhood holidays. She talked excitedly of standing outside the stage door of the theatre, getting autographs of whichever late 1960s or early 1970s star was appearing. We gazed up at the castle, walked through Peasholm Park, and sauntered along the seafront and up through the town, which looked a bit down at heel then, I thought. I remember buying a jacket in Debenhams. Rock and roll.

Before eating at an Italian restaurant she had, as usual, gone to great lengths to look up, evaluate and book, we strolled to Scarborough Cricket Club, where she recalled great crowds of (mainly) men in suits, many of them miners on holiday, heading to watch Yorkshire play during the annual festival.

The entrance was down a gap between terraced town houses on North Marine Road. The ground was empty, of course, when we visited. This was October. As V and I stood taking it in, my memory was of slatted benches curving round one and a half sides of the ground, which felt slightly run-down in keeping with its surroundings. We vowed we would come for a match one of these summers. We never did.

Now, almost five months on from V's death, I decided to go alone for a couple of days to watch York-shire play Surrey at what these days is known by locals, affectionately and self-deprecatingly, as Scarbados. I say alone. There was a gaping hole of physical absence in my life, yes, but a spectral presence in everything I did and everywhere I went, pretty much all the time. Like the sky. Spread over everything. That was surely how grief was supposed to be. That compensating, connecting, continuing presence was the glue that was holding me together, however thinly it might have felt at times.

The 215-mile drive north in June was the furthest I had ventured from home thus far and the M1 junctions evoked emotion enough as I entered Vikki's heartlands.

Junction 30: Sheffield South. The exit for Vikki's family home at Halfway, so called because it was right on the Yorkshire/Derbyshire border. Here she grew up, going to school at nearby Mosborough. She had sold the family home last year to pay for her mum's care at the home in the village next to ours. And because, I'm sure she knew, she didn't have that long and it needed sorting. I was grateful to her that she hadn't left it for me to do. Her mother's ashes were to be buried in the cemetery at Halfway, in her father's grave, said the instructions Vikki had left.

Junction 31: Worksop. My first job on a newspaper, as sports editor of the *Worksop Guardian*. And where Vikki would often go to spend a few weeks in the summer with an aunt, on the tough Manton Estate. A news editor later on the *Daily Mail*, who knew the area, once issued an opinion to the office that V was not to be messed with, having held her own on the Manton Estate. We may even have been in the same town one summer all those years ago, long before we met.

Junction 33: for Sheffield centre, down the Parkway. The main artery into and out of her home city, up which we had skidded coming back in the snow from a Sheffield United v Tottenham League Cup semi-final a few years back.

Junction 34: Meadowhall shopping centre, which featured in *The Full Monty*. Or "Meadowhell", as Vikki called it. Then up over Tinsley Viaduct, the landmark cooling towers there no longer. She once suggested to her friend, fellow Sheffielder Richard Caborn, the former Minister for Sport who still lived nearby, that the city should paint them and make a feature of them. That would have been clever.

Junction 37: Barnsley. Where Vikki carried the Olympic torch for 300 metres ahead of London 2012 and we all went to watch – Alex, Jack, Jean – and were so proud. She took the torch to show the children at our village school and they were touchingly excited, all wanting their picture taken with it.

Junction 40: Wakefield. Where V had her first newspaper job, on the *Wakefield Express*, and won a Yorkshire journalism award for an interview with Enid Hattersley, Roy's mother. She was offered the chance to cover Rugby League for the paper but turned it down as she said she knew nothing about it. Now *that* I would like to have read. And seen her in action in the press box.

Then all those junctions for Leeds. She hated Leeds. Or rather, Leeds United. It was the one thing that Sheffield United and Wednesday had in common. She reckoned that Leeds "stole" her favourite player, Tony Currie, off the Blades. The then Leeds manager Jimmy Armfield would later describe him as the best player he ever signed. Vikki met Jimmy when I went to interview him at his Blackpool home for the *Mail on Sunday* some years later. She forgave him when she discovered he was the nicest man ever to have worked in football and, like me, she became friends with him. She wrote a lovely obituary of him for *The Sun* when he died a year ahead of her.

The M1 became the A1 became the A64 and I bypassed York, where we'd once walked around and visited the Minster, V retracing steps she'd made as a teenager with friends. I would find those photos too in the hoard.

Then there were the signs for Pickering and Whitby. On that trip, we'd eaten wonderful fish and chips at the Magpie in Whitby and ridden the North Yorkshire railway from there to Pickering, buying one of the best fridge magnets in our copious collection. Just before Scarborough came a sign for Filey, where V had spent a childhood holiday at Butlin's. Once in Cornwall, she found a tile with an old image from the 1960s of the pool at the holiday camp and eagerly bought it. It still resides in our bathroom.

Finally, around lunchtime, I reached Scarborough and it wasn't an auspicious start to my stay. My room was at the back of the hotel I'd booked, facing on to some peeling paint and garages. The scene from *Fawlty Towers* went through my mind, when Basil asks the deaf old woman what she expected to see from a Torquay hotel bedroom window. I wasn't expecting the hanging gardens of Babylon, nor herds of wildebeest sweeping majestically across the plain, but I had hoped for a glimpse of the sea. I could almost hear Vikki demanding to know where I had brought her.

The bathroom lights, meanwhile, came with a switch to change from normal to garish cerise. It felt like bordello chic and I wondered what I had booked into. I think V would have insisted we check out and find somewhere else, as she once did on another autumn break in

Northumberland where, rarely, I had booked the hotel. Still, this would do as I would be out watching cricket all day.

Tired from driving for four hours, I took a taxi to the ground on North Marine Road, the driver recommending a place for fish and chips later and depositing me at that opening between the terraced town houses I remembered from my visit with V 12 years ago. I went to the "adults" £18 turnstile but was pointed to the £12 concessions. I didn't realise I was ageing that fast but I wasn't going to complain. And I had missed the morning's play.

"What time can I get in half price?" an elderly man was asking a steward. "Not till 5 p.m.," said the steward to the crestfallen man. I felt sure V would have turned to me and said: "Welcome to Yorkshire."

Once through the turnstiles, it felt like that moment when your dad first takes you into a football ground, that tingly time that Nick Hornby captured so well in *Fever Pitch* when the grass appears in your vision. There were the curved, slatted benches, but I didn't remember all those various stands, all that seating around the ground. Outdated, tatty in places, much of the wrought ironwork rusting due to the salt in the air from North Sea winters, it was utterly appealing. Anyone changing it, like the theme tunes to *Test Match Special* or *Match of the Day*, did so at their peril.

The ground's capacity was listed as 11,500 and it looked about a third full. Plenty of room, but plenty of people too. I was struck immediately by the buzz around the ground. Occasionally a loud laugh would punctuate the hum of voices. Or a shouted remark. My last game had been that day at Leicester a couple of weeks earlier. This was a world away in terms of attendance from Grace Road, and in intensity from the Isle of Wight. This all felt very serious. Serious cricket. Serious cricket-watching.

I sat for a few minutes on the bench seating but realised quite quickly that I was in the equivalent of the home end in football, or more aptly the junior sibling of the notorious Western Terrace at Yorkshire's headquarters at Headingley in Leeds. Here the pints were pulled and enthusiastically consumed on this hot summer Sunday. Empty barrels were mounting up alongside the bar, squeezing up against that standard area for selling old cricket books, resembling a programme shop at Non-League football. Here the van selling pulled pork baps and burgers was also doing a roaring trade. From here would come the barracking for the Surrey players as the afternoon wore on.

I looked for shade around the ground. My skin these days, seemingly as a result of the radiotherapy for my cancer 10 years earlier and various drugs since, was thin and burned easily. There was little in shadow, however. Fortunately, there was a breeze to cool and intermittent cloud cover for protection, and as I got my bearings I found a spot closer to the area behind the bowler's arm. A spot where people weren't drinking and shouting.

I settled down to enjoy some competitive cricket, gazing into the backs of several older men in replica Yorkshire shirts bearing the logo of Wensleydale Creamery, an illustrative cow's head staring back at me. (Replica shirts, in any sport, really do not suit men with pot bellies.) Yorkshire had begun well, with opener Will Fraine making a maiden first-class century, but wickets were now falling regularly. At tea, Yorkshire were a mediocre 246 for seven in what was developing into a good contest. While well ahead in standard, in competitiveness this was more the environment of league cricket, as I had played in Nottinghamshire's Bassetlaw League in my younger days, rather than the Home Counties village cricket in which I had also taken part later in life.

The tea interval was a joy. Dads and lads thronged the outfield for impromptu cricket games. Vikki would have loved the three young girls having a game of their own in the middle of the ordered chaos. Elders gathered at the rope now erected to protect the square, pondering its wear and tear, sagely opining on how it might play later in the game. Gulls swirled, squawked and swooped to fight over dropped chips among the benches.

Meanwhile, I watched a bloke skilfully traversing the outfield from one side of the ground to the other, slaloming through bats and balls, with his two hands wrapped around three pints. Skilfully, that was, until around 20 yards from his destination when a man chasing a Frisbee barged into him and the lot was lost. There were apologies and remonstrations, I could see from 50 yards away.

I wanted to turn to V and say: "Did you see that?" She would have laughed loudly. Or laffed. I could just hear her voice, with its flat Yorkshire vowels, saying: "Ha," before a proper guffaw. How I loved her laughing, and her wicked, even dark sense of humour. It was always such a delight to see her happy, an element of mischief in her eyes. To have made her laugh was to have felt that you'd achieved something special.

The beer-spilling incident seemed to be resolved without violence. It was that sort of a day. England at its best. Nobody knew or cared who had voted which way in a referendum. The crowd – with many more women in it than I'm sure would have been the case here when V was watching men stream to the ground those near-50 years ago – was simply united in its desire to see good cricket and have a grand day out.

Then, of course, as Yorkshire's late order rallied to a respectable total after tea, it came out of a clear blue sky.

Insinuating itself into my psyche, as I contemplated how much she would have enjoyed this, was a vision of Vikki on her deathbed. Her pallid complexion. Her wiry grey hair. The lids closed over her big brown eyes. I suppressed a tear. I wasn't sure how it might look here, though sunglasses and panama hat would have saved my embarrassment. I was concerned that this would be my fate, that whenever I felt at peace, in a scene that soothed me, I would feel guilty and so access sadness as punishment. That sadness alone was my fate. Any sense of enjoyment was still to betray her and her memory. Mixed in was my compassion for her, regret that she was not here to savour all this.

The raucous element on the benches roused me from my introversion. "Your brother's better than you, Sam" came a shout directed at Sam Curran, Surrey's highly promising 21-year-old England Test all-rounder whose older sibling Tom was at the time with England's one-day squad for the World Cup. Curran junior made the mistake of adding to the fuel, of which the heckler was already full, by conceding three consecutive fours off his bowling.

"You're finished, Rikki. Retire," shouted the same bloke whenever the ball went anywhere near 37-year-old Rikki Clarke. Some laughed as encouragement but more grew weary when he continued. And continued. Both factions proved themselves knowledgeable, mind. The heckler knew who these players were. The rest respected them. There was applause from the majority of the home crowd at any good piece of play, Yorkshire or Surrey.

At close of play, I joined the walkers down North Marine Road back into town, stopping on the way for fish, chips and mushy peas at the place the cabbie had recommended. They hit the spot all right. "Not the best in Scarborough but very decent and on your way home," he'd told me. "Mind, all the chip shops are pretty good here. They've got to be; otherwise they close down, there's so many."

It was an up-and-down walk back to the hotel, past the funicular tramway down to the Prom, the views of South Bay and the harbour bathed in evening light. Wearied by the climb up to my hotel, I was quick to fall asleep that night. Would that that had been the end of a full day, however.

Around 4 a.m., I awoke to the thump of my anxious heart. I was a long way from home, from my sanctuary of V's presence. I wondered if this was now my fate, whether life was always going to be like this, and travelling was going to prompt panic. I had learned from experience, though, that panic attacks – while scary and uncomfortable, like the effect of turbulence in an aeroplane – do not last. It may feel that way but they come in waves, then subside. Analysed, they last about a minute. The heart and mind cannot take much more than that and the body returns to its true north for longer periods.

In a period of panic's subsidence, I drifted off for a couple of hours, waking to realise, thankfully, that I would have the *Today* programme now on Radio 4 for company. As I dozed and rested, tutting at wakeful moments at the latest twists in the news, I knew that if I was to fall asleep during the day at least it would be somewhere where it would be appropriate and I would have company in that. At a cricket match.

And at least there was no question of me being late for the start of the second's day play. The more so since I ordered a cab again. I was still a child of that background that considered a taxi a luxury, but they say to be kind to yourself when grieving. Besides, if I was going to walk back tonight, I needed to preserve what little energy I had these days. It meant I arrived 20 minutes before play began and so could bag one of the few seats in the shade I had spotted behind the bowler's arm at the Trafalgar Square end. There was no column here, no sculpted lions, but this Trafalgar Square had a pleasant enough green space at its heart. The other end also had greenery behind it, being the Peasholm Park end, but the stand next to the pavilion had no cover.

There is a tale, perhaps apocryphal, of an announcer once at Headingley, who took to the microphone at 10.59 a.m. "Ladies and gentlemen. Play is about to commence," he boomed. "So stop fidgeting." No such curtness these days. "Good morning, ladies and gentlemen," came soft, well-spoken tones over the speakers. "Welcome to Scarborough Cricket Club and the iconic North Marine Road ground."

Surrey were resuming at 48 without loss after bowling Yorkshire out for 327 the evening before. Getting 375 runs on the board in a day's play – short and quick outfield or not – was no mean feat, and it was shaping up to be a fascinating game. People put down their copies of the *Yorkshire Post*, which was about the only place to get a decent report these days. (The *Daily Telegraph* had just two measly paragraphs in a round-up – of Yorkshire v Surrey, the two giants of the County Championship with 52 wins between them down the years, for goodness sake. And Surrey were the reigning champions.) Others put away their phones, though I noticed that fewer here than elsewhere seemed diverted by them during play.

Yorkshire's bowlers toiled initially to break the opening stand.

"They've just put an extra slip in, and what does he do? Bowls down the leg side," tutted the man behind me. And then he asked of his wife sitting next to him: "Who was that Australian bowler whose wife had cancer?"

Uh-oh. Was there no escape? Just when I was getting over my middle-of-the-night meltdown.

"Glenn McGrath," she replied.

"He could put 11 out of 12 balls down the off side," he said.

"Andrew Strauss's wife had cancer too," she added. "Jonathan Agnew's wife has been having treatment for breast cancer as well."

"That's better," replied the man. "That's pitched up on the off side."

I was in a moment where it didn't bother me, though at another time, for no apparent reason, it might have. I was too tired of feeling bothered currently. And I wasn't going to move and give up this well-won seat. Nor could I get upset at a snippet of overheard conversation when one passing person heading for the toilets said to his companion: "She died in February, you know. She was 88. She had a long association with Scarborough cricket."

Was hearing of cancer and death like buying a red car, perhaps? After that, you see them everywhere when you're out driving. Vikki herself would have been amused at the dialogue and turned to me and said: "Where do you think Alan Bennett gets it from?" (V once came home from visiting her mum, eager to tell me that Jean had said of someone who lived a few doors down: "He's a nice man but he will wear his carpet slippers outdoors.")

Vikki would have enjoyed it, too, when a Surrey wicket finally fell, but that of the batsman on 5 rather than the one on 24, prompting a voice behind to lament: "Well, they've got the wrong one out but it's a start." It might have been V talking.

When something did bother me, it was again out of nowhere, or perhaps more accurately coming from a train of thought where all the carriages were linked. An advert for the Skipton Building Society caught my eye ("When your money's in a good place, so are you"), and I had another moment of wanting to tease V about the stereotype of Yorkshire folk and their money. Very bluntly on the back of the admission ticket, for example, came the information: "PLAY IS NOT GUARANTEED. NO MONEY REFUNDED."

It led on to regrets that we hadn't been here before together, that I had no one to trade insults with. No more would I hear her telling me to sod off, with that smirk on her face and twinkle in the eye, before retaliating with the what-aboutery of my attitudes to money and the slowness on the uptake associated with my Dorset roots. Thank goodness for lunch. Time for the tearoom, with its terrace and sandwiches, rather than pulled pork or burgers.

Once, when sub-editing on *The Guardian* early in my career, I was presented with some news agency copy by a cricket writer covering a match. It read: "In the afternoon session, the batsmen batted and the bowlers bowled." That pretty much summed it up here, except that the fielders fielded as well. I duly dozed, in between doing a crossword. That's the great thing about watching long-form cricket. As the game manoeuvres itself, with the sides spending days doing the groundwork to be in a position to strike for the win on the final day, you can drift off for a while or do something between balls being bowled and still feel engaged with the game.

Tea approached and with it the time for a scone hunt. Vikki was always most professional when it came to hunting scones and I had picked up her techniques. Whenever we were away at a seaside resort or visiting a stately home, she had the knack of getting there before the vicious and voracious coach parties of old ladies who would often clean out cafes of cakes like locusts. I made an early run for it.

On the way, I bumped into some old journalistic colleagues, the retired Pat Gibson of the *Daily Express*,

Michael Henderson, with whom I worked on *The Guardian* and who was now on *The Times*, and David Hopps, a Yorkshireman himself once of the *Yorkshire Post* and *The Guardian* and now of the ESPN cricket website. All offered me their condolences. We reminisced, told stories of old Fleet Street for a while and it dawned on me. This was the only conversation I had had with an adult all day and would do for the rest of the day, as I would walk back to the hotel, gasping for oxygen on the final climb, and be so exhausted that I would have to order room service.

Just before close of play, I suddenly got the urge that was still striking regularly – to ring Vikki, to tell her about how Yorkshire had done. They were on course for a first-innings lead until Rikki Clarke clouted six, four and four consecutively as Surrey made it to 362 all out, a lead of 35. Had there been a heckler – this was a Monday and a more elderly, retired crowd was in – he would have been silenced. Now I wanted to discuss with V the day I'd had and tell her what time I'd be back. To ask her what she'd been up to.

Four years after my father died back in April 2003, I won Sports Journalist of the Year at the British Press Awards. Once off stage after my acceptance speech, I reached into my pocket for my phone to ring Dad before I remembered... I did ring Vikki, who was delighted for me and had said all along after my nomination, amid my pessimism, that she thought I had a good chance. Until I got home and she came out with that Zara Phillips line. Praise was fine, but it wouldn't do to be getting too big for one's boots. Here in Yorkshire today, the episode sprang to mind.

I had been due to spend another night at the hotel and take in all four days of the cricket, but two nights were still my limit away from my haven, our home. I had taken mementoes with me – pictures and that handwritten note from the eve of our wedding – but it was not the same. And so I cancelled my third night. I would instead have a walk around Scarborough in the morning before heading home.

Looking at it more closely now, the town was not as down on its uppers as I remembered it. European Community money had apparently helped – ironic, given that the town had voted for Brexit. The Grand Hotel appeared decent enough again, if not quite grand, having looked faded a decade ago, but now refurbished. The steps alongside it down to Foreshore Road were covered in gull lime, though, and the birds' screeching must have woken a few people up. No wonder I was the only person walking down them, though actually it was a bit early and plenty of places were still closed. Having grown up in a seaside resort, I knew they stayed open late in the evenings, and thus opened up late.

As I made my way to the harbour, a bitter-sweet melancholia descended on me. I was fully aware I was now walking in Vikki's young footsteps. I passed the amusements that she told me her mother and father had frowned upon her going into. I felt a sadness for that little girl, an only child, whose life had ended too soon. Tears welled in my eyes again, but then I could put that down to the wind off the sea.

One establishment was advertising The Sooty Show. The week before, clearing out some old records, I had found an old single by Sooty and Sweep. V had told me that, as a kid, she had got their autographs at the stage door of a theatre in the town. Quite how they did that without ruining the magic for an impressionable child, I'm not sure.

I took the funicular back up into the town for £1 and came across the beautiful shopfront of Greensmith and Thackeray, Colonial Outfitters. It may have been a cafe now but at least it had the grace to keep the old signs. Then, turning left towards the shopping precinct, there was Debenhams, where I had bought that jacket all those years ago because V said it looked good on me. Down a side street now, I found a decent menswear shop where I saw another jacket that I liked, this one rather more expensive. I bought it. It would remind me of Scarborough. And Vikki.

"You here for the cricket?" the woman in the shop asked me. "What's been happening?"

"Well," I said. "There's been two days of everything happening and nothing being decided. If you were an American or you don't like cricket, it would have confirmed your worst opinions. The next two days will decide." She smiled.

I was planning to go to Peasholm Park, where Vikki and I had walked those years ago and she had reminisced. She had taken me to the Pagoda and the Japanese gardens, to the boating lake where mock naval battles involving model boats were staged. I couldn't face any more today though. I was already tired from walking and emotionally drained from the nostalgia and the sadness that, to my relief, the cricket had interrupted. Or perhaps I didn't want to spoil old memories.

I steeled myself for the climb back to the hotel to check out, passing a man on a mobility scooter with a cigarette in his mouth and "Eye of the Tiger" playing loudly on the stereo in his basket. It was a reminder that any pretence that this remained the genteel resort of V's childhood was long gone and that high-season nuttiness would soon be upon the town.

I drove back down the A64, past Kushty's diner and the Kashmiri buffet, and then past all the Sheffield junctions, wondering when I might find it in me to visit Vikki's home city again. Once home I took to my bed. This grief shit, coupled with cancer and the side effects of it, was exhausting. Holding everything together was proving draining.

I followed the match online over the next two days and it turned into a thriller. Yorkshire set Surrey a target of 318 then bowled them out with just 10 balls to spare for 194. County Championship cricket at its very finest; four days of struggle and four hours of exciting denouement. Perhaps it would be enough to tempt me back next year, health permitting. Perhaps this time it wouldn't be too sad to enjoy that walk around Peasholm Park I once took with the grown-up little girl who wanted to show me the places where she'd had fun. Where I'd had fun with her. And glimpses, fleetingly, of fun without her.

· 14 ·

Holiday in Northampton

"This looks like a good spot," Vikki said. We'd got there early to bag a place and we both agreed this worked: 10 yards to one side of the sight screen, looking down the ground, plenty of time to see a ball clubbed towards you rather than being assaulted on the leg side. We settled down in our seats at the end of a row and I went to fetch two polystyrene cups of tea.

When play started and a batsman hit the first boundary, we realised why there had been plenty of room here, even if the seats had filled up as play approached. Four flames from some kind of machine shot up about 20 feet into the air either side of the sight screen. We could feel the blast of heat. Vikki laughed and turned to me.

"Well, it is a bit chilly," she said with a smile.

It wasn't. It was actually quite a warm evening but she was thin these days after another couple of chemotherapy treatments and was off the steroids for now.

It was a mid-August evening less than six months before V's death and we were at Wantage Road for a T20 match between Northamptonshire Steelbacks (named after the county's old regiment) and Yorkshire Vikings.

Yorkshire needed to win to keep alive their chances of a place in the quarter-finals and they did, comfortably. Vikki was struggling physically but happy. She was still making the most of life and had just returned from covering the European Athletics Championships in Berlin. She was being switched from chemotherapy that wasn't working but there were still treatment options left. We didn't know that night that we were just a couple of weeks away from her having to spend nearly four weeks in hospital, such was her deterioration. Nor did we know that we were approaching the endgame.

Almost a year on from that match, I was back at Northampton for another T20 match against Yorkshire. I may not have been in love with this form of the game but I was in love with her – forever would be – and wanted to come to remember, to honour, to cling to a cameo. And just to do something on an empty Sunday. Now, as I sat in my car and thought about that balmy evening the previous July, I mused that so much in life distils into moments that linger long in the memory. I couldn't remember the details of that game that night, but the image of Vikki's laugh flashed into my mind's eye.

And so with sport. In cricket indeed, there had been one just a couple of weeks earlier that would linger for ever in English memories, when Jason Roy threw the ball to wicketkeeper Jos Buttler to run out New Zealand's Martin Guptill in the super over – the champagne super over – that had won England the World Cup after Ben

Stokes's batting heroics had turned the game. Afterwards people talked about how this would boost the English domestic game and maybe attract more people through the gate. (I still thought, mind, that I'd be all right for parking – in a side street at least – and getting into Grace Road on a Wednesday morning.)

I felt I needed to get out and see some cricket again as times had been tough since returning from Scarborough. Going so far from home had required a lot of physical and emotional effort, especially to the county of Vikki's birth and her life before me. It had been pleasant, yes, in so many ways, and the memories warm, as with today's already worthwhile cameo of her smile, but it had also been draining.

As Bruce said when I came back: "When you go to these places, you invite grief in. And the grief triggers the trauma." Post-Scarborough, I grew sad and angry, depressed, not wanting to go out, not wanting the contact of people. Then resenting people for not contacting me. I felt old and overweight, as if life was over for me now that V was gone. I was in God's waiting room with my own cancer – and feeling once more that that might be no bad thing. After all, I was never again going to know and share passion like Vikki and I had.

In my desperation to feel loved still, I tried to remember the things she said to me. "I only have eyes for you, sweetie," she would say sometimes. Tenderly, she'd say, usually after an argument: "I do love you," with the emphasis on the do. (We could even have light-hearted, teasing conflict about that, me suggesting that the "do" implied she doubted it and was trying to convince herself and me.) My favourite – from many years ago, I have to admit – was: "I still go 'wow' when you walk into a room." I always did too with her. Couldn't take my eyes off her.

My downward-spiral mood after Scarborough had been improved only when our friends Tom and Sybil invited me down to the Cotswolds, then with them to Devon for a couple of days. Their cosy hospitality and easy company always lifted my spirits. They let me be me. To be quiet when I wanted, to talk about Vikki when I felt I needed to. Having known and loved her themselves, they could add sentiments of their own. Otherwise, some days doing nothing seemed attractive, and I could convince myself that it was what I needed to restore myself physically and emotionally. In reality, it was simply the lassitude of grief. Another good thing about going to cricket was that, once you had made the effort to get there, you could then do nothing and wallow in that lassitude if it still appealed.

I must have been desperate to get out of the house – or perhaps I had Vikki's voice in my ear about having paid in advance for the ticket and not wasting money – because it had not stopped raining all the way to North-ampton. Play seemed unlikely, but you never knew, and in T20 they only needed to fit in five overs a side to get a result. I knew they would definitely make every effort. This was money-spinning season for the counties and they would have to refund spectators if there was no play.

I parked my car on the same patch of grass where we'd parked last year and, though it was clear there was no prospect of a prompt start, I wanted to get into the ground, to secure a covered seat, to see what other memories might comfort me. I unfurled an umbrella for the five-minute walk and then took refuge in what used to be an old football stand in the days when Northampton Town used to play here. We could certainly all have done with those fire machines today, I thought and smiled anew at the memory.

I recalled coming here for the first time back in the 1980s. *The Guardian* had sent me to cover a Northamptonshire v Leicestershire championship match and I remember David Gower being lbw to Tim Lamb, who would go on to be chief executive of the England and Wales Cricket Board. Gower had been writing in *The Cricketer* about how cricket reporters rarely asked batsmen about their dismissals to gain insight for their writing and so I went to the dressing room and asked him. The enthusiasm of the young, keen reporter. He smiled and indulged me.

The rain lashed on the stand roof now and families around me tucked in to their packed lunches. Mine consisted of pork pies, crisps and Coca-Cola – the usual grief-diet picnic. The DJ did his best to lift spirits, playing "It's Raining Men", "Why Does It Always Rain On Me", "Take It Easy" by the Eagles and "Gangnam Style". He certainly lifted mine by playing – if a little incongruously – Neil Young's "Keep On Rocking In The Free World".

With no play going to happen any time soon, I had plenty of time to think and my mind wandered to summers of previous years and the holidays that Vikki and I had taken together. And those we had not. That's the thing about grief sometimes. On good days, the mind's pictures from the past are gorgeous but on bad days those pictures taunt you with your loss. Today was a better day, thankfully.

Vikki was an intrepid traveller. Going places sustained her soul. I was more of a homebody. She loved the relaxation of a long-haul flight with its chance to read books and watch films. I, someone who had attended no fewer than three "fear of flying" courses in his life, spent my time listening to every whirr and buzz of an engine for signs that we were going to crash. I somehow endured the anxiety for the sake of my job, including a World Cup in the United States that involved 14 internal flights as well as two transatlantic ones, but short haul was long enough for a holiday's sake.

And so we reached a compromise, almost an unspoken one. We would have a week together in the summer in Europe when there was no football and, more importantly for V, no athletics to cover, then a week in

England, usually at a nice seaside or country hotel, in the autumn. Come midwinter, Vikki would head for somewhere exotic on a group, guide-assisted trip. She made lasting friends on tours to South America and Bhutan, Kenya and Myanmar, some of whom came to her funeral. Nobody fenced Vikki in and, while I may have had my daft moments, I was not going to be foolish enough to try.

In her absence now, I wished I'd gone with her to some of those places. Often she would ring me late at night from far-flung locations, when she could get a signal, telling me of her day and what she had done. I especially recall her regaling me with tales of Angkor Wat and Machu Picchu. I think I probably lamented that the washing machine was on the blink or that some 21-year-old footballer had turned me down for an interview for the Sunday paper I was writing for.

We did have one marvellous, memorable midwinter trip together. In 2016, sensing that time was running out for a couple with cancer, I made a suggestion that we go together to somewhere I always believed I should visit before I died. Vikki readily agreed. And so, 10 days before Christmas, we took off to Jerusalem and the Holy Land for four days.

It was a magical time. V being the smartest of travellers, after landing at Tel Aviv, we got to immigration first and were quickly through to pick up our driver so that we could check in to our hotel (the historic American

Colony on the edge of East Jerusalem; V had made the booking) and were soon at the Western (not technically, apparently, the Wailing) Wall to watch the Jewish ritual of Friday-evening prayers.

On the Saturday morning, we were up early, walking through the narrow, enclosed streets of the old city, eerie and closed, to get ahead of the crowds at the Church of the Holy Sepulchre, to which all evidence points as being the site where Christ was crucified. Soon it would be crowded but for now we were third and fourth in the queue and were able to get in quickly to see the tomb, where they let people into the confined space six at a time. Returning to the hotel in time for breakfast, we had what we both agreed was the best cup of coffee we'd ever tasted.

Over the next couple of days, we walked the Via Dolorosa, the way of sorrows, with its 12 stations along which Christ bore the cross on which he would be crucified, from the courtroom where he was sentenced to his death on Calvary Hill. We sat and drank tea on a roof terrace that gave us an astonishing view of the whole melting pot of the old city and its four quarters controlled by various branches of Christian, Jew and Muslim.

We marvelled at how people lived so closely together in its crowded pedestrian alleyways. So often we would see items on the news relating to violence here – there had been incidents of Jews having their throats cut in public, in daylight, in recent months – and of course in

Palestine. Being here, we quickly grasped the tensions, as armed soldiers guarded all the gates of the old city of Jerusalem, but we were surprised, too, at just how people divided so intensely by religion managed to coexist.

We hired a guide to take us to Bethlehem to visit the site where Christ was born, the Church of the Nativity, but as an Israeli, he had to leave us at the edge of the city. We were then picked up by a Palestinian Christian guide and posed for a picture in front of the giant Christmas tree in the square. Vikki then decided she wanted to walk down Star Street, to the concern of our guide, who had a car waiting and was worried about our safety, but this was Vikki he was dealing with.

He was a young man, resentful that his religion was marginalised here in Palestine and his access to Jerusalem's holy sites so restricted.

"I read the Britain First website," he said. "Is that a good website to get a picture of your country?" he asked.

"Er, no," Vikki and I replied, glancing at each other and trying not to look too horrified.

After he had delivered us back to the city's edge, our Jewish guide then took us to the river Jordan to bottle holy water and from there to the Dead Sea, where we both had fun floating in the highly salted water. As we checked out of our hotel, Tony Blair, still a Middle East peace envoy, was checking in. Even V, who had travelled everywhere, agreed that it had been a marvellous experience, one of the best trips of her life.

What stuck with me most was a stroll around the Garden of Gethsemane and sitting in a small chapel alongside it in peaceful contemplation. Genuinely, we both agreed that we felt some kind of spiritual presence here. It was here that the gospels documented that Christ had prayed the night before his crucifixion, here where Judas had betrayed him.

It was here also that Vikki took the picture of the olive tree that was said to be 2,000 years old, stones at the base of the tree arranged to form the word Peace, a picture she made into the Christmas card that so comforts me and remains on our sideboard at home.

Otherwise, our favourite places were France – autumn or spring breaks to Paris, summer to the South of France – and Italy. Often she would complain that it was left to her to book the holidays but it was just that she had such an eye and taste for good hotels and restaurants that I could not even attempt to match her choices. She knew best. Really, she did. It was best just to let her get on with it.

She found the pretty little hotel in Antibes that time we saw Keith Jarrett at the jazz festival. It was not far from the villa owned by my friend Tony Adams, of Arsenal and England fame, that he lent me once to take Alex and Jack, and where V joined us to meet her future stepchildren for the first time. Tony, having come to love France, had bought it after the 1998 World Cup. It was near Mougins, in a location on the hillside recommended to him by Patrick Vieira and Thierry Henry.

It was idyllic and we had a marvellous few days, but what I remember best is Vikki arriving by taxi, work having kept her in London for a couple of days after we had got there, to find us locked behind security gates that had become stuck. That was not going to stop her. She simply threw her suitcase over and clambered over them despite wearing a short skirt. God, she looked magnificent.

Years later, she also found a beautiful hotel just above Gore Vidal's house in Ravello, near Naples, on a clifftop and where Greta Garbo and D.H. Lawrence had stayed. Not together, though. I think. Now they would have made some couple. (This was the hotel where they played Barry White at breakfast and I made V laugh by sashaying across the dining room to fetch her coffee. She thought I looked like the Hofmeister bear.)

As these times sprang to my mind, my gratitude grew at the holidays and breaks we shared, and the little images to be treasured. There were some not so great, mind, as Vikki would also point out. Though the kids loved it, she hated the Mediterranean cruise – one of the few holidays I did book, which is probably why I stopped – and being cooped up in a cabin at sea. Fortunately she did enjoy better our other whole-family trip when the kids were teenagers, to Boston and Cape Cod, especially baseball at Fenway Park and whale-watching off Provincetown.

Then there was Bruges. I suggested we have a long weekend away to celebrate 10 years of life together since her diagnosis, and she chose there. We did all the things we should, took a boat trip on the canals, sat in that magnificent square. And I recall her ballsily chiding half a dozen British kids for getting pissed and upsetting locals who were baffled by their behaviour on the train back to Brussels and the Eurostar.

Whenever I sat at cricket and thought of us together on holiday, though, I always thought of a little Mediterranean fishing town on the Ligurian coast of Italy near Genoa. And today, as the rain pelted the roof of this old football stand, I pictured how it would be at this time of year when we would take our week of sunshine in what became the most beautiful of boltholes for us. Unusually for Vikki, once we discovered Camogli, we kept going back. She liked variation, to find new places, but this became such a special place to us that every January, once the holiday ads started to appear on TV, she would say that the magnificent hotel she had found back in 2014, and which we came to love, had a deal on if we booked early.

"Yes, let's go for it," I would say.

"Well, we know we like it, don't we?" she would reply. It became a rite of the New Year.

We would book a taxi from Cristoforo Colombo airport, crossing the bridges built across valleys – including the one that shocked us and the world when it collapsed in a rainstorm in August 2018, just a couple of months after what would prove to be our final visit –

and negotiating tunnels carved into the hillsides. Then the cab would descend into the town with anticipation and the knowledge that a peaceful, glorious week was stretching out ahead of us.

The Hotel Cenobio dei Dogi was a little faded but full of charm. It had the most beautiful view from the top of a cliff gazing down on the small town with its shingle beach of coloured parasols, a venue we would discover that also played host to the childhood holidays of Roger Federer. The pool was warm, the terraces well-furnished and you could always get a sunbed. The rooms were not luxurious but airy and comfortable. After the first year, we got to know which had the best views and so each January, when she booked, V would request one of them.

There were three restaurants and for lunch we would always – I mean every day – have linguine vongole and a strawberry panna cotta. By day, Vikki would sunbathe and swim, and I would avoid the sun and swim. We would both read. She would get through a book a day. In the evenings, we would stroll into the town and peruse the book and souvenir shops, sit with a drink or an ice cream. Here she bought me a leather bookmark with my initial on it, which I treasure.

At least once during the week, we would take the ferry to the cove and monastery at San Fruttuoso to lunch at Da Laura, the gorgeous restaurant that inspired Ruth Rogers' menu when she founded River Cafe. I still have the picture of Vikki's face in my mind as she sipped a complimentary, strong limoncello there with a mixture of a wince and a smile. I hastily took a picture that is now at the centre of my kitchen montage.

During our first year there, we took a trip to Portofino for a morning, to visit the town made famous by such celebrity lovers as Richard Burton and Elizabeth Taylor, Wayne and Coleen Rooney. But never again. It quickly filled with coaches and cruise ships debouching and we couldn't wait to get away, back on the bus to the small town of Santa Margarita, where I had stayed during the 1990 World Cup when I was covering the Republic of Ireland for *The Guardian* and where V now found a little clothes shop with Italian cuts that fitted her perfectly, and thence to Camogli.

So much did we love the place that we even contemplated buying a flat there. It was less than two hours' flying time from London, and the airport at Genoa was never crowded so planes were rarely late. It was then 20 minutes in the car to this hidden gem, less popular than the busy Cinque Terra towns but favoured by Italians.

Sometimes, if I'm honest, I worried a little that Vikki and I might grow snappy with each other when it was just the two of us away together, spending 24 hours for seven days in each other's company. She was used to a lot of company, thrived on it, on her travels for work or midwinter recharging of the batteries. Rarely did we argue, however. We had time, away from the daily grind, to realise why we loved each other. We became the best version of ourselves for the other. The memories were warm and I was grateful for them.

It was all certainly a far cry from Northampton on a soggy Sunday, though I'd re-engaged with that happy memory of a year ago here. At 3.05 p.m., the umpires decided that the rain was not going to relent for long enough to get in even five overs a side and so we all trooped out of the ground back to our cars. Five miles south of Northampton, wouldn't you know it, the rain stopped and the sun came out.

It was frustrating and annoying but such is cricket; such is life. At least I'd had an afternoon out, had a picnic, been occupied by a crossword and brought to mind those happy holiday snapshots amid all the rain. When I got home, I cooked some pasta.

· 15 ·

Twenty Questions

. . . .

Having missed out on an afternoon at T20, I thought that maybe I ought to give it another go this summer. And it was a way of spending more time with my son Jack, who may not have been willing or able to take the "excitement" of eight hours or so of a County Championship game but might just have been able to endure three hours of tedium of 40 overs combined.

That much had been proved back in 2003, on 13 June to be precise, when he was just 13. My then newspaper, *The Observer*, sent me to The Oval to cover the first night of this newfangled competition, Surrey against Middlesex, and write a piece about the experience. Young Jack was the target audience, after all, as the game sought to attract a new generation who had not grown up with the game so embedded in their culture as mine, possibly due to the decline of cricket – an expensive and time-consuming sport – in schools. He enjoyed it. I thought it was too short a match.

Tonight it was Middlesex v Kent at Lord's. The top two in the Southern Group. These days, T20 matches were as much social events as sporting occasions and had become fixtures of the London summer. The "Home of Cricket" was duly packed, almost to its capacity of 30,000. It would be an astonishing sight, an example of the haves and have-nots in the county game when compared to Northampton. Such was the state of the modern sports press, however, that it would merit just a few paragraphs in the broadsheets the following day, and nothing in the tabloids. To them, this was a routine, nightly, occurrence with little of news value, I suppose.

I met Jack early at the North Gate so that we could get something to eat and make the most of the welcome early-August evening sun at the Nursery End. There, you could sit and watch the players warm up, go through their fielding drills. On what grass was left at the Nursery End, that was, what with all the new tented pavilions. They used to play matches here back in the day, even if the boundaries were short, but there was no longer enough space. At least the ground had escaped a scheme a few years back to sell it off for yet more ridiculously expensive flats in leafy St John's Wood.

These days, you needed almost as big a mortgage to buy the food from the various outlets. The queue for fish and chips was too long and so we settled for a chicken curry that emptied the pocket but barely filled the stomach. We would need something else later. Still, I wasn't going to worry too much. I was with my son at cricket – cricket of a sort – and if all wasn't well with a world in which Vikki was not, then this was about as good as it could get in the circumstances.

What surprised me most was the champagne bar at the hub of all the refreshment venues. I don't recall seeing one of those at Wantage Road. And it was doing a roaring trade. Lord's tonight appeared to be a recession- and austerity-free zone. I thought of the vintage bubbly that Vikki's brilliant oncologist at the Royal Marsden, Professor Ian Smith, had sent us on our wedding day. As I didn't drink, it really belonged to her and she had always been saving it for a special day. She'd thought she would share it towards the end, when visitors would come and celebrate her life with her over canapés and fizz, but it hadn't worked out like that. She was too ill, slipped away too quickly. The bottle still lay in its ornate box in a cupboard.

Kent won the toss and it was enjoyable to watch them bat. Back in that very first game in 2003, Middlesex had made 155 all out in exactly 20 overs, a total Surrey chased down for the loss of eight wickets with four balls to spare. More than 300 runs, and 18 wickets falling in an evening. Everyone thought these were remarkable totals, of almost eight runs an over and a wicket every 12 balls. It had been the same in the early days of one-day, 60-over cricket, when five an over seemed extraordi- nary to those used to maybe three an over in the County Championship. Nowadays, those 20-over statistics were below par. Kent made 204 for four – 200 not too long ago was seen as an imposing milestone but it was reasonably common these days – and the feeling was that Middlesex could chase this down, especially with the brutal South African A.B. de Villiers and England's rampant World Cup-winning captain Eoin Morgan in the side.

The atmosphere around Kent's innings was enjoyable, too, as the ground was still filling up. So too was the crowd, not least with bubbly. And as the Middlesex innings unfolded, so many in this audience unwound.

This was not really a cricket crowd. It was more a cross between a stag or hen do and a Friday night in the City as the traders uncorked their take on the week and its computer-screen tallies. As the night wore on, fewer and fewer of them watched the cricket and yet fewer of those seemed to care. Even just around us in the Compton Stand – and multiply this around the ground – there was a group of exhibitionists wearing caps from a cricket club in Hertfordshire making a din, along with a work outing fuelled by pints and Prosecco and oozing gossip, resentment and sexual politics. Now and then a champagne cork would pop to loud cheers. Apparently, trying to hit a fielder in the deep with a cork is a "thing" at London T20 matches.

I found the using of Lord's and cricket as an extension of a pub quite depressing. There was nothing specifically nasty about anyone, just an arrogance to some people, a sense that it was acceptable to behave this way; loudly, brashly and with little sensitivity for those nearby. There seemed to be little of the healthy shame (toxic shame being a much different matter that I would not wish on anyone) that we are supposed to feel to stop us making spectacles of ourselves.

I gazed on the dozen – white – boorish blokes in cricket caps chanting drunkenly and grunting look-at-me noises, and tried to imagine what people might have thought had this been a dozen black or Asian lads. Would they have received the same indifferent indulgence? I suspect not, which may well be just one reason why you don't see much of it in public, certainly not at sporting events.

Was I a spoilsport? An old curmudgeon? Had I turned into some bore who lamented – as did the ageing in every era, probably – the lowering of standards of behaviour in public to the point it had become a new normal? Who cursed the fact that nobody in authority seemed to care much these days as long as it stopped short of violence and people spent their money on a hedonism that subsidised "proper" cricket?

Or was I just a grieving man who did not know any more what fun was? And maybe would never again? That thought alarmed me. But then, detaching from the omnipresent alcohol that seemed to take over the evening rather than become an accompaniment to it, I enjoyed spending an evening with my son. And enjoyed the game in which I took an interest, until it began to peter out.

Losing wickets regularly, Middlesex were never really in the hunt. Too much was asked of the big guns

De Villiers and Morgan, and after they fell following too brief a scoring flurry, Middlesex limped to 176 for seven to lose by 28 runs.

Despite that, all evening, at boundaries or between overs, those in charge of the music did their best to keep the atmosphere lively. And though the catchy tunes were largely wasted on me, it seemed to do the trick. And even I could not help smiling when "Sweet Caroline" came blaring out of the speakers around the ground. The Neil Diamond hit had become almost an anthem for T20, the perfect singalong song. My smile was because it reminded me of a warm memory of Vikki, me and the kids at Fenway Park in Boston watching the Red Sox take on Kansas City Royals a dozen years earlier. The song became synonymous with the seventh-inning stretch at baseball games, when the crowd would be urged to get to its feet for some movement, and it seemed that English cricket had appropriated the idea.

The DJ this evening had saved it for near the end, along with "Hey Jude", when the mood was flagging and the game was done. It had given me an idea. As Jack and I spilled out on to Wellington Road with the rest of the crowd, I decided that 6 August, less than a week away, was going to be a music day to mark six months since Vikki passed.

· 16 ·

Ain't There One Damn Song...?

The role of music for those who grieve, having spoken to so many who have experienced loss, seems to become central in their lives. We all have songs that resonate, that echo meaningful moments, that mirror moods. Somehow they take on more depth after the death of someone close. Music had been hugely important in my life ever since I was a teenager who got a weekend job in a record shop. Now it became vital.

There's a line towards the end of "Young Americans" by David Bowie, when the music stops and he wonders, yelling almost plaintively, whether there's "one damn song" that can make him break down and cry. For me, this became more: ain't there one damn song that can make me *not* break down and cry?

Back in the spring, to sidetrack me from the craziness at weekends that had begun in the March, I decided to sort through our CD and record collections. Well, now I had the time to get the piles of material, on shelves and in cupboards, into some kind of order. I had been promising myself for years that I would do it. And my first discovery was that we'd brought to the relationship about 50 "doubles", albums that we had both bought. That, I thought, was a comforting sign of how much we had in common. The second copy of them all could go to the charity shop. So could plenty more old compilations, stuff that I would never play and that was just occupying space.

There was also stuff that I would never play but with which I was never going to part. That single by Sooty and Sweep, "Sooty's Concert" (featuring Kipper and Butch, it said on the sleeve; we mustn't forget the brilliant Kipper and Butch, though they often went unappreciated back in the day). Then one from when Vikki must have been around 11 years old, an old acetate – a floppy plastic record – that was obviously a giveaway from a magazine and entitled "David Cassidy Sings and Speaks". She had such a crush on him when she first began to notice boys, she told me. She had even designed a sleeve for it. It was precious to me now. As was a single she loved from that era that she had lost but a copy of which I had found on the internet for a recent birthday, "White Horses" by Jacky.

Maybe I thought music might go some way to filling the emptiness. Inside me and the house. And I thought that, if I was going to play it more often now, I would treat myself to new equipment, including a shiny new turntable, speakers and amp, so that I could enjoy my old vinyl – my listening medium of choice – and any new music I planned to buy. My son took me to a specialist shop he knew at the back of Oxford Street and helped me choose the system. It was a thing of beauty and offered me something to look forward to.

Before it arrived, however, having sifted through the wealth of mine and Vikki's back catalogue, I wanted to assemble in order on shelving all the material in sections that suited my tastes. First I put closest to hand those that had meant most to her and me, then my 20 favourite albums. After that, greatest hits albums and finally, the rest in alphabetical order. I knew quickly where to find the relevant sounds that would catch my mood. Would remind me of her. Of us.

Some people clean their way through grief. Others find other obsessions. Food. Pets. (Getting a "grief dog" is a thing, apparently.) I took the bloke's route and rearranged my record collection.

The first album I played when my new sound system arrived was Neil Young's *Harvest*, mainly for the track "Out on the Weekend" with lines burned into my soul, about loving and being loved by a woman who was gone but who was still calling. Then it was Joni Mitchell, probably Vikki's favourite artist, and *Blue*, probably her favourite album. Oh, I thought sometimes, I wish I could skate away. I found a new souvenir edition of the LP, in blue vinyl, in a record shop.

After that, every Saturday morning afterwards for months, I would play them along with that Keith Jarrett album and a melancholy, haunting vinyl LP my son had given me, *Spirit of Eden* by Talk Talk. Not forgetting *Cole's Corner* by Richard Hawley. I saw online a new edition of it with the vinyl in orange. It being her favourite colour, I just had to have it. It wasn't just because the title track was the first dance at our wedding reception. It was his best album. How wonderfully evocative it sounded as it played loudly on the turntable and I shed tears of grateful sadness.

That probably wasn't "our song" though. That would be something altogether livelier to represent V: "The Look of Love" by another Sheffield act, ABC. One Christmas, I had the lyrics printed and framed as a present for her and she liked that. She put it on the wall by our bed.

Now, on my music day to mark the sixth-month anniversary of her passing, I went through other significant songs and artists from our life, starting with Van Morrison and Bruce Springsteen, recalling concerts we had been to. Van was our first together – another at the Albert Hall when the grumpy old bugger performed *Astral Weeks* live was the most memorable – and Bruce our last. That was at the Ricoh Arena, Coventry. I loved that she loved how much I was enjoying my favourite rock musician, standing up, singing along, doing a bit of dad-dancing. I particularly liked the young lad a few rows in front, standing and singing every word of songs written long before he was born. It was like seeing a next-generation supporter watching your favourite football club.

I also put into the CD player, as I often did, Brahms Violin Concerto, played by Anne-Sophie Mutter. We had been to see her play it twice, at the Royal Festival Hall and the Barbican, and it always brought a tear to my eye as I recalled those occasions. It was V who introduced me properly to classical music. I may have teased her sometimes about some of the rubbish, as I saw it, on her iPod but she did have eclectic tastes.

Somebody on Twitter a couple of weeks earlier had set a challenge: tell a story with a three-word song title. So how many did you want? "She's Not There" by the Zombies was the first that sprang to mind. Then "Lost Without You" by a new artist called Freya Ridings that I was playing a lot. I just couldn't avoid "Nothing Compares 2U" (well, it's three words written like that). V had once sent me a mix cassette tape led by the Sinead O'Connor song (written by Prince) during a period when we were apart. It was another way of saying she wanted us to get back together and through the tears I smiled. Oh, those lyrics, about somebody being gone and being able to do whatever you wanted now. Except that there was nothing I wanted to do now. About how living with someone could be hard but still nothing compared. I thought more and more about regret and wasted time. Why was I putting myself through this? It was, I guess, the necessary wallowing of the grief-stricken.

It was never going to stop there. Indeed, it set me off on a morning of sitting at my laptop, finding songs on You Tube, one leading to another. Starting with one-word titles, led by "Stars" by Simply Red, about falling from the stars straight into a lover's arms. She used to play *Simply Red Live in Cuba*, mainly because she'd been to Cuba on one of her winter trips. That led to me looking up the photos on her phone of her, in a fetching and appropriate retro summer dress that I had suggested she buy at a seaside shop in Southwold, sitting on the back seat of an old American gas-guzzling car that takes tourists on trips of Havana.

And then on to two-word titles. "Without You" by Harry Nilsson, followed by "Fix You" by Coldplay. It became a song with a lot of meaning for us when I was chairman of Weymouth Football Club (and Vikki was inspiration at my side, even vacuuming the carpets in the sponsors' lounge before the first home game of the season). We would play the song, with its lines about lights guiding you home and galvanising, as I drove over the hill into the town, from the top of which the sea would come into view to greet us.

Now the sentiments about tears streaming because of losing something irreplaceable brought a lump to the throat and reminded me of the closing ceremony of the Paralympics in 2012 when Vikki had got me tickets to see Coldplay in the Olympic Stadium and I went with

Alex, texting Vikki as she sat in the press seats. As the song added, today I felt too in love to let it go.

On to four-letter titles. "It Must Be Him" by Vikki Carr was the starting point. That was her dad's favourite singer and why she was named Vikki. Then "Wish You Were Here" by Pink Floyd. "I Want You Back" came next. "She's Like The Wind" by Patrick Swayze followed. Why? Early on, when I'd first met her and thought about her a lot, there was a haunting and daunting line about the singer feeling a fool to believe that the object of his affection would see anything in him. Some time later, though, I must admit, there were times when that line from a Buzzcocks song about falling in love with someone you shouldn't have fallen in love with went through my mind.

After that, a free-for-all. "I Love You Always Forever" by Donna Lewis. It was a cheesy song, and Vikki knew it, but she liked to sing a line about my blue eyes at me. My heart would melt anew and I'd sing back that Edwyn Collins song about never having met a girl like her before.

Mind you, she didn't much like it, that time back in 2007, when she was losing her hair through her first chemo and had decided to have it shaved off and I sang a version of the Bee Gees' "More Than A Woman" to her with the line changed to "bald-headed woman". She came to see the funny side, though. I thought she looked great with her head shaved.

I played "Every Time That You Walk In The Room" by The Searchers, as a reminder that we'd gone to stay with our friends Tom and Sybil, to see the 1960s band in Stow on the Wold during their final tour the October before Vikki died. She was frail, just a few weeks out of hospital. She struggled so but came because I wanted to go.

Then stuff that Vikki had introduced me to: Mary Chapin Carpenter's "Passionate Kisses" and Natalie Merchant singing "Don't Talk", the best song about alcoholism ever written. Natalie Merchant. My goodness. I came to love the 10,000 Maniacs singer's version of "Every Day Is Like Sunday" and pretty much anything else of hers on YouTube. It had to be on YouTube. She looked so much like V. Danced, a bundle of energy, like V. I also, in this summer of cricket, raided Vikki's Roy Harper collection for "When an Old Cricketer Leaves the Crease". And I couldn't resist playing "Shine On You Crazy Diamond".

Some were good, even wonderful songs, others... not so much. They were just songs that prompted memories, provided the soundtrack to our life together. I couldn't take too much more of the intensity, but I couldn't finish without the greatest evocation of loss of all: "Who knows where the time goes?" How had life got to this point? One day you're a kid setting out on life full of hope and fear, the next you're a widower contemplating what's left of it with regret and fear. All the worthwhile stuff in between – the love, the achievements, not least of helping to bring up two great kids – counts for nothing on a day like today.

After the eponymous line, Sandy Denny also sang about who knows how love grows. When the music stopped that day, I realised that mine for Vikki was growing too. Only in death once the everyday is no more, somebody once noted, do you discover the reservoir of feeling for someone close. I hadn't expected that either.

· 17 ·

After the Boys of Summer

It was to the airs of classical music that Vikki's mother Jean died, just under seven months after her daughter, on Monday 2 September 2019, at the age of 89. Apart from a couple of hours when a care assistant thought it a bit too gloomy, the radio was tuned to Classic FM as accompaniment to four days of Jean slipping away. Like Vikki, it was a peaceful passing with, as far as could be discerned from the bedside, no obvious pain.

I had just completed my Friday ritual of laying two long-stemmed roses on Vikki's grave and was about to drive to Southampton to stay with two of our friends, Richard and Emma, when the call came. Jean was weakening, the care home said. She was not expected to last the day.

It had been four years earlier when Vikki and I brought Jean down from her Sheffield home to a home that understood and could deal with her vascular dementia. The home was in the next village to us, which meant we could be nearer to her and thus visit more easily. I have to admit that I had found it difficult, upsetting, visiting on my own these past six months and more, though it was a little easier when I went with Vikki's friend Moira, who had become Jean's too, as well as mine.

The worsening of the mother of the woman I loved served as a reminder of my loss, but I knew that I owed it to Vikki to ensure that Jean's last months, and now days, were as comfortable as they could be. And so I stayed with her as she gradually slipped into unconsciousness, holding her hand, talking to her about our beloved Vikki. She was in no position to question where her only child was. Jean had, apparently, last asked about V some eight weeks earlier, wondered why she hadn't been to visit, but a minute or two later had moved on to another subject.

I'm sure at some level that Jean knew Vikki had died. In his novel, *Here We Are*, Graham Swift uses the word "goneness" to describe the state felt by a widow, and I felt just that in this room now. Had Jean been able to articulate her feelings, I think she would have said what I wanted to say too. Basically, we both just wanted Vikki there with us. Perhaps V was here, as some people said that she always was in some form when I lamented her absence, but only in our own home did I really feel any sense of her presence.

Which is better? (Or worse?) To be conscious of the pain of missing the closest person in your life, or to be unconscious of it? Tough call. In one way, I envied Jean the latter. But it was the only way. I decided that I was grateful for the pain, as perverse as that sounds. The depth of my grief was in proportion to the depth of my love for Vikki, I had come to see, and I was keenly aware of that love. With that, came a depth of pain that I wouldn't have traded.

Jean died on the Monday lunchtime, the quiet death that Vikki would have wanted for her. She would have been as relieved as I was. The task now was to organise another funeral, my second of the year. This one, though, was an altogether less demanding one to arrange. As might be expected, Vikki had left instructions. The service for Jean was to be in Sheffield and her ashes were to be interred in the grave of her husband, Fred.

About 30 family and surviving friends turned up despite the lashing rain and it was, as Vikki would have wanted it, simple and touching. I gave a eulogy to the mother of the woman I pined for, recalling our wedding day when Jean teased the chef because the Yorkshire puddings were not up to the standard the county expected. At the end, the coffin exited to the strains of Glenn Miller's "Moonlight Serenade". I could just picture Jean and Fred meeting at Coles Corner in Sheffield on black-and-white 1950s Saturday nights, a kiss and a hug before a night out in the city.

Afterwards, the nearby hotel where we had held Jean's 80th and 85th birthdays put on a buffet for mourners, a hotel that had been derelict when Vikki was a child and that spooked her walking home from school in the winter dark along an adjacent lane. I couldn't help thinking of Vikki joking about Northern funerals and "big baps", but the hotel provided neat sandwiches. As I drove home with Moira, I felt proud that I had done right both by my mother-in-law and my wife.

By now, the football season had begun and I'd started going back slowly to watch Non-League games locally. At one, Hemel Hempstead Town against Bath City, I bumped into an old friend of Vikki's, Matthew, a Bath supporter, whom she had known from her time working in Bristol so many years ago, and to whose wedding we were invited. I wanted to get out my phone, to click on Vikki's number and say: "V, you'll never guess who I've just met…" It still happened regularly. Before I remembered.

I was still more interested in the cricket season, and the finale of the County Championship was approaching. Before the long months without it, I wanted one last day of reflection with the game as backdrop and I decided on Surrey v Nottinghamshire at The Oval. Why? Probably mainly because of the man who had kept me alive this year. Bruce's consulting room had been in his house on Kennington Oval for many years and, before they built the new stand at the Vauxhall End, you could see the square from his garret window. I often used to walk up the wind tunnel that was the Harleyford Road in mid-winter and dream of sunnier days watching cricket.

It had been at The Oval a week earlier that England had beaten Australia to level the series at 2-2, the Aussies thus retaining the Ashes but England enjoying a decent series. As with the World Cup, it was Ben Stokes who had captured the public imagination, notably in the third Test at Headingley, when he made an astonishing unbeaten 135 – his 10th-wicket partner, Jack Leach, making a single – as England recovered from a first innings of 67 all out to win by one wicket. It was one of the most remarkable Tests of all time, one to rival the Botham–Willis heroics at Headingley in 1981.

I contrived to miss the phenomenal Stokes innings, of course. With England nine wickets down, still 73 runs short of the 359 victory target, I decided that Sunday afternoon to go to the pictures for the first time since Vikki died. It was to see a film entitled *Blinded by the Light*, based on a true story about a young boy of Asian heritage growing up in Luton as a fish out of water by liking the music of Bruce Springsteen. It was a shocking decision, not just because I missed the greater drama and spectacle of the Miracle of Headingley II. It was awful being in a cinema but unable to share moments with V, not hearing her whisper an observation about the movie in my ear (which used to annoy me at times but that I would happily be annoyed at now), not being able to show off to her that I knew all the words to the Springsteen songs, to discuss it all on the way home with her. Instead, I just cried as I drove back.

I'd felt strange on my own in a cinema. Like a gap in a mouth full of teeth. I noticed couples everywhere, felt very alone, sensed that people were looking at me and judging me as a pathetic loner and loser. Almost certainly, all that was going on only in my head, but I would not be repeating the experience any time soon.

The thing about going to cricket on your own is that it doesn't matter if you are among fellow loners and losers. Nobody affords you a second glance and you don't feel conspicuous. At The Oval today, there were plenty of similarly single men dotted about, sensing the last of the summer wine, plenty of us with snow on the roof or thatches in need of repair. I took a seat at the Pavilion End, contemplating the Vauxhall skyline that resembled Dubai these days with all the high-rise development going on, and watching the planes going overhead to Heathrow as we were under today's incoming flight path.

There was also a group of schoolkids being led by a teacher who probably liked cricket and, having decided that herding cats was worth the trouble for a day out of the classroom, had somehow persuaded the head that it was a good idea. Rod Stewart's line about it being late September and really needing to be back at school went through my head. At first excited, the kids soon grew bored. I was reminded of a story a cricket reporter friend had once told me about being at a Lancashire v Sussex game back in the 1990s when a small girl, clearly dragged along by her father, had complained of being bored on a somnolent afternoon of over after over of leg spin.

"Bored? Bored?" her baffled father had wondered. "How can you be bored when Ian Salisbury is bowling to Michael Atherton?"

There was a chill in the air today, a day for fish and chips at lunch (there wasn't much else on offer, actually), but some of the Surrey batting – admittedly against a limp Nottinghamshire attack continuing to labour to season's end – was warming. Ollie Pope, who would make his maiden Test century for England against South Africa in the winter, and Scott Borthwick both made tons as the bat dominated.

It meant I could drift away, had time to take stock of how I was doing. Better than I had been, for sure, but still prone to regression in periods of deep sadness, forcing me to retreat into the four walls of my home. Our home. That was where Vikki still resided, as far as I was concerned. Not a chair didn't have a picture of her within vision.

I was trying to get out more. I bought tickets and went with a friend to Chelsea v Liverpool and enjoyed a sociable day. I went to stay in the Cotswolds again with Tom and Sybil. I felt safe, comfortable, there with them. They took me to a lovely village fete and to an open day at Adlestrop racing stables where the amiable Richard Phillips trained his horses. I ended up taking an eighth share in one, to Sybil's approval. "You need to start doing things for you, Ian," she said. It still felt a bit early. I couldn't be enjoying myself when Vikki couldn't, after all.

Today, rather than getting out, it was time to get in more. The rain began to fall on The Oval to force an early tea and that was that. I was glad to get home ahead of the London rush hour and out of the wind and the rain heralding autumn.

The teams would be out very little over the next few days either, probably to the relief of both, given that their seasons were fizzling out. Underachieving Surrey would make 420 for six declared and woeful, relegated Nottinghamshire 73 for one. "O Trent Bridge, weep for shame!" wrote my former colleague Michael Henderson in *The Times*. "That most handsome of grounds turned into a theatre of base comedy."

Fortunately, the story was less dreary and drizzly elsewhere, even if only a little, and I had begun to take an interest again in the wider game rather than just my days out. At Taunton, it came to a final match between Somerset and Essex to decide the winners of Division One of the County Championship. It might not have been quite the epic of Liverpool v Arsenal as the last match of the football season in 1989 when both could win the old First Division title, nor even Middlesex's dramatics to win the 2016 County title on the final evening, but it contained excitement all its own, with Essex holding out for a draw and condemning Somerset to the runners-up spot for the third time in four years. You felt for them.

The season was sliding out of view (to borrow an image from another of Vikki's favourite bands, Sheffield's Pulp). The clocks would be going back soon. Darker evenings were on the way. We were six months from any more cricket.

Over the summer, I had read much about the county game and its potential demise. The articles and observations were by journalists and critics – who were also lovers of the game, those who wanted it to succeed. There were debates on the state of pitches, the Championship being shunted to either end of the season when it was too easy to take wickets and too hard to make runs, on whether the County game was preparing players for Test cricket, or whether young players were simply interested in one-day rewards rather than four-day fulfilment. Even whether it could survive financially when the real money was in the one-day game, including the new format due for the following season, The Hundred.

Me? I felt a bit as do visitors to Bath, where V and I had stayed a few times and where we had taken the kids on an outing when they were in their teens one half-term. While locals may feel that the city is losing its architecture, charm and history, the tourist is surprised at how much remains. Arguments about the extended game of cricket and its obsolescence had been going on for nigh on a century, yet here it still was.

Even before this season, I had always felt a sadness when the cricket season ended. That was without even attending, just following the scores and watching the odd game on TV. The mere knowledge that it was there in the background was always comforting. A tradition, a part of my Englishness, my culture and identity, were being maintained in a changing world.

In this year of living with the breath of sadness, actually making the effort to go to cricket, and sitting watching its intricacies, had been a huge source of solace. I didn't want to go every day. But I wanted to go now and then when I felt the need. Cricket didn't talk back to me and it didn't offer advice. It didn't tell me what to do nor how to feel. Like a best friend, it was just there for me, willing to embrace me and allow me just to be, whatever mood I was in. I desperately hoped that it would continue to be there for other souls in need of balm for the spirit in the future.

As Bruce had suggested, I had given it the cricket season. Was that that? Of course not. It hadn't cured me, hadn't really changed my life. I was still bereft, a widower, alone. So much was still to be endured. But it had been there all summer when my grief was at its zenith, and I would never forget that and the debt I owed to the game.

A song went through my mind – "The Boys of Summer" by Don Henley – and felt fitting. My love for her was still strong, long after the boys of summer had gone.

·18·

Learning to Limp

Today is 7 February, one year and one day since Vikki died. I couldn't write yesterday. I just wanted to honour the first anniversary of her passing in peaceful reflection, by sitting for a while on the bench that I'd had made to be sited close to the foot of her grave. As on the day of her funeral, it was unseasonably warm. I read and pondered, looking up occasionally to marvel at the recently installed, beautifully elegant headstone of Welsh slate I'd commissioned and which told of my pride in her in words that marked her life. And mirrored it.

In the morning, I went to buy flowers. Orange, of course, with red and white roses for Sheffield United, who were doing remarkably well in the Premier League, even touching the top four. Outside a nearby shop, I saw a man smoking. I recognised him. He was a grumpy guy who worked in a small newsagents and I'd seen him smoking along this terrace for 20 years or more. He must be in his seventies now. Or looked it. I wondered how he'd got away with it, how he got to survive when my Vikki was in the ground.

Unfair, illogical and way outside my control. But I couldn't help thinking it and feeling angry. I calmed down in the peace of the cemetery at God's Acre, arranging the flowers with the sun warming my face. The daffodils that I had planted in early November with Matt Biggs, the *Gardener's Question Time* panellist who lived in our village, were beginning to poke through. Moira arrived to plant snowdrops and crocuses. We talked about Vikki's last day, the day of her death 12 months ago today. I said how privileged I felt to have been present with her throughout the 12 years of her illness, to have been there at the death of the love of my live.

There was now a sweetness to my heartbreak, I noticed. I had loved deeply. I had been luckier than most people in life. That which friends had told me, I began to believe.

Afterwards, I spent half an hour in the church where we were married and her funeral took place, contemplating, lighting a candle for her. And I went home, cooked a meal and had an early night. As I had so many times over the past year, but this time without the anxiety and panic attacks that so often accompanied the night's onset. I was sad but thankful. Today at least, as I now looked back on the past year and its feelings and events, I was not as crazily sad as I had been intermittently for so much of the time since Vikki's death.

If the widespread and heartfelt reaction to V's passing surprised me, what happened next over that first year astonished me. Tributes and awards were never far away from her. Nor was I. Leaving our home, with her omnipresence, was a wrench, though gradually I became braver, venturing further afield both physically and emotionally.

The Sun were true to their word and announced The Vikki Orvice Scholarship for a female sportswriter. They whittled down the entries to a shortlist of six, and I was part of a panel who interviewed them before settling on a young woman who not only had the enthusiasm for the job, but a smart sparkiness that echoed Vikki. Isabelle Latifa Dean quickly settled in and, at 21, was soon covering Premier League football.

I suspected that our village book festival, Books in the Belfry, of which Vikki was co-founder and responsible for booking the authors, would die with her. Before that happened, I wanted to honour its memory, and hers, and put on an event in her name. I noticed that Simon Thomas, the former *Blue Peter* and Sky Sports presenter, had a book about grief coming out entitled *Love, Interrupted*. So sadly, he had lost his wife Gemma in November 2017 to a blood cancer at the age of just 44. I made contact, we met up and he agreed to appear in our local church in the autumn of 2019. I ordered the book and devoured his honest story of coping with his own pain and that of his then eight-year-old son Ethan.

It was a remarkable night, our packed church hanging on his every word. Everyone, after all, has lost someone, and Simon's communication skills, his speaking from the heart, touched everybody present. The event also came at a timely moment for our village. There had been – staggeringly, in our quiet rural community – a murder and our night was a small way in which we could come together. At the end of the evening at least, even if I would feel an emotional hangover in the subsequent days after bearing my soul in support of Simon's self-disclosure, I felt we had done V proud and created an experience by which people could remember her.

I spent a lot of my time, and was grateful for the opportunity to fill it in such a way, in perpetuating Vikki's name and legacy. I had been overwhelmed at seeing just how much she meant to people – surprised at first, because we were just Ian and Vikki getting on with our lives, doing our jobs, writing our stuff – though it took me a while to accept that I had to share her with others. I guess I had shared her during her life, but it hadn't felt that way. I resented it at first – echoes of my trauma of wanting her exclusively – then realised what a force for good her public profile could be.

I contacted her old comprehensive school, Westfield in Sheffield, at an opportune moment to see if they might like to mark her achievements in some way. The head teacher emailed me back to say they had just decided to reclaim a large working area to re-establish a library. It was a sign of the times that they had lost their library; hopefully a more encouraging sign that they wanted it back. And they wanted to call it The Vikki Orvice Library. She was, said the head, exactly the kind of person and character they wanted young students, especially young adult females, to use as inspiration.

I offered a donation to help stock it with books, and even took up some produced by my small publishing company to start a sports section. V would have liked that. The school wrote to the comedian and children's author David Baddiel, who was doing a book signing in Sheffield, to see if he would open the library and he agreed. It was another emotional day, he and I having a moment of reminiscence about Euro '96, when he and Frank Skinner were No. 1 in the music charts with "Football's Coming Home", and one of the best summers of both our lives. It was, after all, the summer when Vikki and I first really connected.

The bench I had ordered to sit in the cemetery, inscribed "In Memory of Vikki Orvice/She Loved This Village", took three months to make and arrived in the autumn. Because it takes pretty much a year for the earth in a grave to settle, however, there was little point ordering a headstone until a few months before the anniversary. I browsed the brochures provided by the funeral directors but could see nothing that fitted for Vikki. Most seemed just so, well, cheap. Besides, I could not decide what to have inscribed. All Vikki had wanted was her name and dates. That felt too stark for me. My wishes should count for something too.

I did some research on the internet, and following a visit to a churchyard in the Cotswolds that our friend Sybil had said contained tasteful headstones, I decided on Welsh slate. I had an idea, too, that I wanted something inscribed that would convey not only how loved V was, but also how influential, something that would capture both the personal and the professional. I also had the sense – without wanting to be grandiose on her behalf – that there might be young women visiting this grave some time in the future and I wanted it to have gravitas. And class. With a flat vowel a, of course.

I found an engraver in Oxfordshire whose work and website looked impressive, and so I made an appointment to drive over, with Moira as my second opinion. Giles was perfect. He made the clever suggestion that to make the stone distinctive, he might engrave it both front and back. And so we settled on, at the front:

VIKKI ORVICE

1962–2019

Treasured wife
and daughter
Trailblazing
journalist

Then on the back:

> Greatly
> loved,
> widely
> admired

It was a work of art. When it arrived a few days before the anniversary of her death, seeing it in situ had me blubbing again. I just kept finding new ways to shed tears. I would leave instructions in my will that my headstone, to go in the plot adjacent to Vikki's and which I had reserved, was to match.

As Sybil had urged me, I did try to do the odd thing for myself as well. The racehorse in which I had taken a stake, Lady of Authority, made its debut over hurdles at Stratford and I made my own debut as an owner, enjoying the lounge and access to the parade ring and a private box. Lady was 11th of 14 in the novice race. This was equivalent of lower-division football and a lot of fun.

That enjoyable early-autumn day out was an interlude; one that offered hope, but an interlude nevertheless. Still the madness could return, out of the blue, and fear would overwhelm me. Yes, it was still the fear of stuff I didn't know about Vikki's life but I must have been making a little progress as it had gone beyond just that. I had, after all, long ago stopped looking at her diaries and quizzing her old friends.

It was Bruce who got me to see it during a revealing session about the dynamics of trauma: "Once traumatised, the big issue for a person is the fear of being re-traumatised," he said. "And inadvertently, the fear of being re-traumatised creates another trauma."

When would there be escape? Never, it seemed, only a learning to live with it, of learning to walk with that metaphorical limp. A night-time crossword and Radio 4 would help get me off to sleep, along with lavender spray on the pillow, but for much of the year, anxiety and the dead of night was only ever a few hours away. Progress was fragile.

It was in a session with Bruce, nine months exactly after V's death, on 6 November, that an unexpected turning point arrived. Or was at least signalled. It was a particularly down day. This wasn't getting better, I told him. I just could not see an end to it. You can talk all you want about time and patience and letting the process take its course, but I just couldn't go on feeling as shit as this for much longer. It was two days before what would have been Vikki's 57th birthday and, though I tried hard not to project how I might feel on any given day, I wasn't looking forward to being reminded of past years when I would take her out to nice restaurants for a treat.

Bruce asked me to take him again through my pain at discovering the diaries and photographs back in March. Of how it echoed my angst from childhood and teenage years that came with feeling then that I had been abandoned emotionally by those who had been closest to me. I was reluctant. I really didn't want to go back into any of this. It was just too distressing. But Bruce is a counterintuitive therapist and says the antidote is often to be found in the pain itself. To understand the trauma, he believes, and thus come to terms with it, requires revisiting it and feeling it. It's like that kid's story about going on a bear hunt: you can't go round, over or under it. You have to go through it. An hour of tears later, I spilled into the street, walked in a trance to my car, drove home on autopilot, had an early night, trembling as I turned out the light, but slept for six hours straight for the first time in about three years. Probably due to emotional exhaustion.

The next day, I received a phone call from an old friend and contact of Vikki's by the name of Jackie Brock-Doyle. Jackie was Lord Sebastian Coe's right-hand person, had been with him all through the London Olympics, and again now that he was president of World Athletics. Seb, she said, wanted me to accept on Vikki's behalf the President's Award at the World Athletics Awards in Monaco at the end of the month. I would be sent a plane ticket and be put up in a top hotel. This was quite something.

I was humbled and grateful. But when the call ended, I really didn't want to go to Monaco. I hadn't been abroad since Vikki died. I didn't want to feel alone for a weekend, bumping into and facing up to so many people in athletics that V had been close to, a couple of them names in those diaries that she had been on "dates" with, had dinner with, at times when we were not together. It was her world, not mine, and apart from the odd trip with her to athletics events, I always left her to it. I'd even had trouble watching the sport on TV over the summer. I rang Bruce to say I didn't think I could go. He told me just to think it over for a day or two.

On the morning of Vikki's birthday, I checked my social media feeds and saw that Facebook had put something on my timeline. "Together Down the Years" it said, followed by a series of pictures of V and me that we had both posted over time. It was accompanied by some tinkly piano music. Blubfest did not begin to cover what happened next.

Of course, I realised that these were just highlights. Moments of joy. Lovely as they were, naturally they didn't tell the whole story. I looked at one, for example, taken in a restaurant with us happy, smiling and well fed. And I recalled that on the way there, we'd had a bit of an argument. I can't remember what it was about or what started it. Were we late? I think so. It might have been that she was still working on a story, or I had been on the phone to somebody for too long, and we had risked losing the reservation. Or did I not want to go out as there was a decent football match on telly? But then, that's Facebook, where everybody's life looks so shiny until you meet them for coffee and the conversation starts. It's like a highlights reel on TV of the big hits at a T20 cricket match. All very exciting at the time, but too many of them simply diluted the pleasure. And they covered up the bad bits, as when a result was predictable a long way from the finish. True love for the game was about enduring all the boring, routine bits as well so that the highlights meant so much more. So it was with relationships. The mundanity and conflict were to be savoured too as part of the whole story (and God, I realised, what I wouldn't give for a good argument with Vikki now), as was sometimes doing things one of us didn't want to do for the pleasure derived from seeing the other person happy.

I thought of Vikki, Monaco and the award. She would have been glowingly proud to receive this. I could just picture the look of delight on her face. She was not one to take things like this for granted. She savoured any nomination, let alone the winning of an award, and it was so joyous seeing her excited about them. And this was about her, not me. I needed to face this, to go, and be her representative. To make a speech on her behalf. To act with dignity.

I rang Bruce to tell him about how I was feeling upbeat today on Vikki's birthday – again, not how I was expecting to feel; ain't life just like that – and said that I thought I should go. He was pleased I'd arrived at that decision. Something, I felt, was beginning to shift. I was starting to feel if not exactly better, then at least less bad.

I still didn't trust it. It felt precarious, tenuous. I felt I could go back into panic mode at any time. But I think making what for me was a bold decision to go to Monaco offered the first inkling that I might be moving forward rather than getting stuck, and it felt all right. Whatever "all right" was going to be. Right now, anything but anxiety and debilitating fear would be all right with me.

Bruce told me that he believed something had changed for the better in our session two days earlier as well. He said he believed I was being told in my heart that I needed go to accept this award and face my ghosts. Soon after our call had ended, he texted: "Treasure that realisation, Ian. It's Vikki's birthday. Love is bigger than trauma. Love is letting go of fear. Buy something today to symbolically represent this so you see it and acknowledge it every day. Love you, Ian."

What did I buy? A book on trauma and addiction. I knew how to give myself a good time. "That wasn't quite what I meant," he said with a smile when I told him at our next session. "But at least you bought something."

Before that, there were other commitments. In mid-November came the fruition of six months' planning. I had been approached by some friends of Vikki's – journalists and broadcasters Jacqui Oatley, Carrie Brown, Jo Tongue, Mike Collett and Philippe Auclair – wanting my blessing for a dinner in Vikki's memory. We could raise funds for the Royal Marsden, they said. I readily agreed, though would have my wobbles over the summer when I wondered if we could pull it off, despite *The Sun* agreeing to sponsor it. We settled on Lord's as the venue. It seemed fitting, given my season of watching cricket. V had also liked going there to British Sports Book Awards dinners.

I was worried about whether we could, between us, sell enough tables or badger enough people to donate auction and raffle prizes. I was worried, too, if I am honest, that people might tell stories and have memories of Vikki that I didn't know about and didn't want to hear. On a couple of occasions in our monthly planning meetings, I had to leave the room in an emotional state.

I needn't have worried. I was lucky enough to be surrounded by Vikki's colleagues and friends on the committee, who were both professional and sympathetic. I quickly came to see how Women in Football had succeeded as a collective: egos to one side, eyes on the prize. What unfolded, as also followed after the news of Vikki's death and the attendance at her funeral, was quite astonishing. Sports clubs and organisations were more than generous. Wimbledon donated two tickets for the Ladies' Singles final. Mo Farah gave the vest, signed, in which he ran the London Marathon, and the London Marathon itself donated a place in the race for a runner. Gary Lineker offered a behind-the-scenes experience at *Match of the Day*, and Arsenal, Tottenham and others gave signed memorabilia, as did Anthony Joshua. We ended up with some 50 auction lots and 20 raffle prizes.

We comfortably sold 40 tables of 10 too, to organisations, clubs and private individuals. My friend Steve Claridge, conducting the auction of the five biggest-ticket lots with Vikki's athlete friend Kath Merry, said he looked across the room and could not see an empty seat. I had been to plenty of dinners down the years and so often people booked tables just to show goodwill but then couldn't fill them. There was usually an empty chair or two on many tables. This room was full. And it was full of a warmth I had never before known in my long experience of these events.

Jacqui Oatley hosted, brilliantly. She had also edited a short film about Vikki that had us all blubbing. I had suggested Emeli Sandé's "Read All About It" as the music, remembering it from the London 2012 opening ceremony, because it so fitted Vikki. The film included footage of Vikki being interviewed by Gabby Logan for a BBC documentary about sexism in football and contained footage I had never seen. Because I knew Vikki so well and knew how she worked hard to hide it, I could see how nervous she was. Now I had moving – in both senses of the word – footage of her. Later at the dinner, Gabby and the Olympic gold-medal long jumper Greg Rutherford spoke beautifully about V, how her interview skills and charm often left him worried that he had said too much.

I gave a short speech, saying that it had taken me a long while to realise that other people besides me were missing her too. And that, though people die, love doesn't. I thanked the Royal Marsden staff – 10 of whom were here, thanks to their table being generously paid for by my friend Jimmy Mulville of Hat Trick Productions – and they received a standing ovation.

Above all, what was most touching to me was the sight of so many young women in the room. We had agreed with Women in Football that there would be 30 tickets heavily discounted for those who could not afford the full price, and they were snapped up. Our triple aim of celebrating Vikki, inspiring young women and raising money for the Marsden was realised and I felt blushingly proud. In the end, we grossed £103,000 and the Marsden charity staff talked of naming a consulting room at a major new centre on the hospital's Sutton site after Vikki.

A week later, I was asked to present the Inspiration Award at the British Athletics Writers Association annual lunch to a representative of James Ellington, a sprinter who had recovered from a serious motorcycle accident to run again. Vikki had interviewed him on several occasions. She had also won this award – the only non-athlete to have won it – in 2016. Now BAWA had decided to name it after her.

Then came Monaco and the World Athletics Awards. I flew out – nervously; my first time on an aeroplane since V passed and the first time in years without her – very early on a Saturday morning. The South of France was almost under water, with rain lashing and having done so for the past few days apparently. Indeed, it would not stop hosing down for the whole weekend.

I was given an enormous room with a gorgeous view of the Mediterranean, even if conditions meant visibility of only about 100 metres out to sea, and all my meals were provided. At lunch, Seb sought me out to welcome me. I told him how overwhelmed by all of this I was.

At the event itself, in the Grimaldi Forum, Prince Albert of Monaco sat in the middle of the front row. I was just behind, on the end of a row, ready to receive the award. There were several hundred people in the hall, among them the cream of the sport from around the world. Seb took to the stage and gave a short introduction to a video compiled about Vikki. I would never take such tributes for granted, but I was getting used to them. And I didn't want to be too emotional when I took to the stage, as I had a few words I wanted to say on Vikki's behalf.

Then came Seb concluding the video with: "She loved life, she loved athletics and she loved Ian." After that, when the lights came up, I was called up to receive the award, and there were eight women standing in a line on stage. At this point, I did grow emotional. They were all colleagues of Vikki's, either in the media or public relations, who, Seb said, had all been inspired by her. They included Kath Merry, Jackie Brock-Doyle and Jayne Pearce-McMenamin, all great friends of hers. Vikki would have been so touched, above all, to think she had been an inspiration to fellow women professionals.

I fought back tears as I had to go into professional mode myself – for Vikki – to receive the award from Seb and make a speech. I told of how her fellow Sheffielder had inspired Vikki's love of athletics as a teenager, of how she'd persuaded *The Sun* to back the London Olympics, which was instrumental in getting the public onside for the bid. The Games had given Vikki the finest moment of her career and showed our country at its finest, I said. I told of how I grew prouder of her with every passing month, and added: "The sport of athletics was good to Vikki. I like to think that Vikki Orvice was good to the sport."

Afterwards, I was shown into the VIP reception and there I bored Prince Albert with the story of the night Vikki phoned me from Singapore on the day London was awarded the Games in 2005 to say that after Seb's presentation to the International Olympic Committee, the Prince had asked a question about Weymouth (how far was it from London?), which was my home town. He politely told me that he had indeed gone to Weymouth in 2012, and I told him that the TV coverage of the sailing there showed the sea to be much bluer than I remembered as a kid learning to swim in its freezing, battleship-grey waters.

I thanked Seb for this award again, for his lovely words about how much Vikki loved me. "She did. She really did," he said, nodding. I grew emotional yet again.

A tweet from the actor Reece Dinsdale around the time summed up what is felt by so many who mourn:

"This grief thing is bitter sweet. I put up a story of my Dad standing up for the women in the factory where he worked and it got a most overwhelming reaction from thousands of you. I felt SO proud of him. And then I felt his loss more acutely. You can't bloody win, can you?"

The next day after the awards, though, I flew home feeling much lighter, a little more confident that the shift from darkness to shafts of light might be more than just fleeting. I had, as Bruce said, stared down some ghosts. While I still felt her loss acutely – and hoped I always would – I began to feel that, though I might never win, I didn't have to keep losing.

A test of that feeling came over the first Christmas without V, which was always going to be daunting. I was determined to go to the Royal Marsden carol service at the front of the building in Fulham Road this year. Last year, she had been too ill to make it, which she worried might be bad luck after 11 years attending, but she simply wasn't up to it. This year Moira came with me and we bumped into lovely friends of Vikki's. There was Kaz Mochlinksi, part-time sports journalist and full-time Marsden oncologist, who had helped us so much down the years, as well as Ka Wai Ko from the charity department, who had been part of the organisation for the dinner at Lord's. Caroline, the wife of the great sports writer Hugh McIlvanney, who had been a patient here too, also came up to say hello. Hugh had died just before Vikki and we had regularly encountered him at the Marsden.

While there, I also bought a Christmas wreath for the door from the flower stall on the corner near the hospital from where Vikki always bought one. It cost a fortune but was worth it. After the Twelve Days of Christmas were over, I would lay it on her grave.

Otherwise, I could not stomach going through a Christmas the way I traditionally had with V. I imagined getting the decorations down from the attic and putting them on the tree. She had always liked to do that. Everywhere in the world she went, she bought two things: a fridge magnet and a tree decoration. I couldn't face seeing them again and being reminded of the emptiness. And so I decided to rent a house for a week and invite some of Vikki's closest friends for part of it, my family for the rest. We could all get together, remember Vikki and swap happy memories. I would not have to be surrounded by my loss in my own home. I searched online and found a place in Sussex with an indoor swimming pool. I needed to do something different. Swimming on Christmas Day would be different.

It proved to be perfect. Vikki's university friend Emma and her husband Richard from Southampton came, as did my son and daughter, Jack and Alex, and their partners, Carmen and Rich. We ate well – Alex and I sharing the cooking of the turkey and trimmings duty – walked, swam, played silly Christmassy games and enjoyed each other's company.

Inevitably there was a blip. I was up far too early on Christmas morning and was suddenly left with my own thoughts in a big, quiet house. I soon felt her absence acutely. I wanted to drive home, back to the house where, in my eyes, she still resided. It was Alex who talked me out of it, told me that Vikki was with us here. We would toast her over lunch.

On Boxing Day, I took them all to Dungeness, that bleak spit of Kent coast where a power station dominates and, in a wooden shack, the filmmaker and painter Derek Jarman had once lived. Vikki and I came here several times and I wanted to show her stepkids this place unlike any other in the country. The wind howled, whipping up the waves of the grey sea, and we walked on the shingle. We loved it. I was so relieved that what could have been a painful time became an uplifting one.

Coming home to a lonely house for New Year could have been depressing and it worried me. But after so much company over Christmas, and having moved from loneliness to a greater understanding of being alone, if not always at peace, I sensed a glimpse of acceptance of my lot now, of valuing my solitude, punctuated by the company of a few close friends. People did drop away – for whatever reason: weary of your grief, wanting to allow you space or whatever – but that was now OK. I was becoming quite "single". And so on New Year's Eve, I had no desire to go out and join in the revelry.

Actually, Vikki and I together never did. Instead we would usually go to one of our local beautifully restored picture palaces, The Odyssey in St Albans or The Rex at Berkhamsted, where they would show an old movie – something like *Singing In the Rain*, which we had seen the previous year.

It did, though, give me an idea. I decided to watch at home her favourite movie, *Some Like It Hot*. We must have watched it 10 times together. One Christmas, as a present, I bought her a souvenir Taschen edition of memorabilia (in a big orange box), including black and white stills of scenes and a copy of the typewritten script. I got it out from a cupboard on New Year's Eve and reminisced, smiled and cried my way through the beautifully written and acted comedy, thinking of her all the while. She loved most the scene on a train where Jack Lemmon and Tony Curtis, now dressed as Daphne and Josephine, join Sweet Sue and her Society Syncopators to play "Running Wild" with Marilyn Monroe singing.

A few weeks later came another remarkable, moving tribute to Vikki. I was invited by Arsenal – always a classy football club, no matter their then travails and the distractions elsewhere with his American sports franchises for their owner Stan Kroenke – to the Gunners' game against V's beloved Sheffield United at the Emirates Stadium. And not just invited to the game. Accompanied by a friend of Vikki's from Women in Football, Mie Østergaard, first stop was the press room, where they had affixed a plaque in Vikki's memory to a desk that was reserved for the day in her honour. A Sheffield United press official had also put a Blades scarf on the chair, which I would wear for the afternoon (and put on the back of her chair in her office when I got home later than night). I had to take myself off to the gents to remove a speck of dust from my eye. Then it was up to the directors' lounge, where I was handed a personalised programme with "In loving memory of Vikki Orvice" printed on the cover.

This was how only the wealthiest could afford to experience the game. The food was, quite simply, the best I have ever had at football – oysters, no less, followed by fillet steak. I thought of all the sausages and chips I had eaten in Non-League boardrooms, and purred with pleasure. The seats in the directors' box were heated, and there were blankets to cover if the chill still bit.

Ten minutes from time, Blades grabbed an equaliser for a point and I was up out of my seat, as were the Sheffield United directors and dignitaries two rows in front of me. Among them was Tony Currie, and I couldn't resist having my picture taken with him. How Vikki would have devoured the experience, even if she always felt her spiritual footballing home was on the John Street side – then a terrace, now seating – at Bramall Lane.

(Come the March a couple of months later, I would even go there and dine in style. The ex-athlete and London Marathon director David Bedford had successfully bid at the Lord's dinner for lunch with Tony in the lounge on John Street for a game against Norwich and generously said I could have it. It was another magical day that V would have loved, as Liz Byrnes, a Blade and sports journalist friend of Vikki's I had invited, got to sit with TC to watch the game.)

Around this time, prompted by Sophie Hannah planting the seed in my mind on that crime-writing day course where I sought refuge, I also went back to university. I duly applied for that Master of Studies in Crime and Thriller Writing at Cambridge and, after an interview in the summer, I was accepted. There was a wobble in the autumn, not long after Vikki's mother died, when I phoned Sophie and told her I was having second thoughts. I was tired of death, I said, and it was the central element of crime and thriller writing. She told me to think again for a month or two, adding: "It'll be a lot of fun, too." Really? And if it was, I was worried that I didn't want fun. Didn't deserve it.

But I did give it a go. As Bruce repeated, and as I'd learned down the years, life and success were often simply about showing up. I attended the first four-day residential course of my Master of Studies at Madingley Hall with 17 other students of all ages, and became a member of Selwyn College at a small, smashing dinner with the college Master, Roger Mosey (once of the BBC, who had overseen their 2012 Olympic coverage), and senior fellows. It was time, as my friend Sybil had said, to start doing things for me as well as for Vikki. I enjoyed the irony of qualifying for both student and senior citizen discount.

Then came that first anniversary of V's death. As I had been steeling myself for that, I was ready for the emotions it threw at me and made the right decision by spending it mostly alone and in peaceful reflection. I contemplated the house, our house, to which I had had much done over the year, in accordance with how Vikki wanted it. Now I could not even think about moving from this place in which she was still everywhere. I still couldn't bring myself to move her clothes from their drawers and wardrobes. Those draped on her chair in the bedroom, I asked Moira to move and she put them in a suitcase and stored them.

Then there was the final "first" anniversary: 26 February, marking one year since her funeral. I looked back now and could scarcely believe that a year had flown by. And dragged. The shortest, longest year of my life. The most beautiful church service I had ever been to, apart from my marriage, in the same place, to Vikki. I marked the day again with flowers everywhere, at the grave and in our house. As I contemplated that funeral service, I was comforted by the knowledge that we had given her the best possible send-off.

A while later, a plaque would be unveiled at the entrance to our church. It noted that a new church door had been made possible with a sizeable donation in her memory. It was one final, fitting, formal little something that I could do in her honour. Along with the bench in our cemetery, it meant that her name would be kept alive in our village. That was on top of being kept alive in the worlds of media, sport and cancer care. Hopefully too, in the world at large. "She certainly made her mark," a cousin of hers said at her funeral.

To me, a year and a day on, she remained – would be for ever – the woman and the lover whose hair I was privileged to brush for the last time.

Postscript

. . . .

Over the first winter after Vikki's death, cricket continued to play a big part in my life and my recovery not from grief – after all, it isn't an illness, just an inevitable part of life – but from the insanity of grief. That was what most took me by surprise and that, it seems, is what is least talked about. Surely I can't be alone among those who grieve, or have grieved, in thinking that I was going over a dangerous edge from sadness to madness?

I observed the "draft" for The Hundred and wondered what the heck was going on, how Joe Root could be assigned to a team playing at Nottingham or Johnny Bairstow to one in Cardiff (I could just hear Vikki bemoaning a structure that meant that Yorkshire's best players were playing outside the county). I wondered too how cricket lovers in the South West could be expected to travel to Wales to support a regional team for whom their allegiance would be tenuous.

I watched as much as I could of England's tour of New Zealand. Despite the poor performances and series loss, it was still soothing to see the game being played – in sunshine, too, when at home we were enduring cold, wet and darkness. And more wet. The game was a reflection of that shaft of light poking through into my life, both literally and metaphorically. I recalled an interview I did years ago with the head man at Sky Sports, Vic Wakeling, who later became a friend and who died a few years back, that England playing cricket in the Caribbean had been almost as instrumental as football in selling satellite dishes in the early days.

After the New Zealand series, the South African tour was altogether more enjoyable as England recovered from losing the first Test to winning the next three with the irrepressible Botham-for-our-times Ben Stokes leading the way, and most of the rest of the team having a moment in the sun by contributing handily. It was something that got me up in the morning and for that I was grateful.

And I pored over the County Championship fixtures when they were announced. The competition was, as expected, pushed even further to the margins of the season with the arrival of The Hundred, then the T20 tournament following that at the height of summer, but I began to plot another itinerary: Sussex were at home to Durham on opening day this year, which would fall over Easter. Tempting. Sadly, there was no first-class match on the Isle of Wight, just a 50-over match in the watered-down Royal London Cup between Hampshire and Lancashire in August. Scarborough in June this year was due to play host to Lancashire. The Roses match.

Now that was alluring. Yorkshire would be the visitors to The Oval for the final match of the 2020 season.

Then came the dreaded and dreadful COVID-19 virus to Britain, which did for all that. Did for everything. The Hundred was postponed a year, and cricket was left hoping at least to fit in the Twenty20 tournament and some Test matches just to rescue the season. I found myself bereft again, with the mixed feelings of isolation; grateful for my fortunate environment of our house and garden but, marooned in it all the time, more aware than ever of the bitter-sweetness of Vikki being everywhere and nowhere in it. Of course I would have given anything for her to be back with me, but I was relieved she would not have to worry about treatment, the coronavirus and her compromised immune system, nor the care home plight of her mother. I felt fortunate that at least, unlike many, I was there at Vikki's bedside when she died, then free to organise a funeral to which so many came. When a friend died of the virus, I "attended" the online funeral, sad for his widow whom no one could approach to console.

Even before the lockdown, I read a lot. Not just "grief" books, such as those by C.S. Lewis and Joan Didion, but books on love. Vikki had given me a Julian Barnes book, *The Only Story*, to read on our last holiday in Camogli and I read its opening paragraphs time and time again. I thought it quite the most beautiful beginning to a book ever.

"Would you rather love the more, and suffer the more; or love the less, and suffer the less? That is, I think, finally the only real question."

My answer was always the same. My life with Vikki had been an example of it. I was, now fog was clearing more than a year on, grateful that I had had the time with her, punctuated as it was by conflict that made the making-up so much more intensely sweet. I was often reminded that the depth of my grief was a reflection of the depth of my love. More friends told me that we were lucky to have found something together that few people did in their lifetimes. I grew more open to such comforting thoughts.

I have to say, I also read some nonsense. "We don't miss people. We only miss the memory and feelings they gave," somebody wrote. Er, no actually. I miss Vikki. Her as flesh. Her voice.

It would be fanciful overstatement to suggest that cricket saved me that year after Vikki passed. Whatever I had done or not done, I would still have felt the pain – the denial, the bargaining, the anger, the depression. That is, if I had been willing to endure it rather than avoid it by finding some way out through not accepting treatment for my cancer. But it gave me a destination and an activity, a peaceful place where I could grieve in solitude with humanity still at hand. If I wanted, I could be distracted by the game going on in front of me, by its subtleties unfolding, or I could retreat into my pain, to feel it, experience it, and work my way through it. Nobody need notice and that was how I liked it. And cricket rewarded sticking with it. Those uninitiated might wonder what the heck was going on at first but gradually understanding its intricacies induced a comfort. It was a mirror in that, too, for grief.

I was relieved that the County Championship still existed that summer and felt for those for whom it would not, could not, be there the following year. I hoped that its absence would be mourned and that, when cricket returned, plenty of room would continue to be found in the schedule for its enduring virtues of patience and persistence. The virtues that Bruce had urged me to embrace in the early days after Vikki died.

I, for one, would forever celebrate it henceforth. As long as there were people like me in need of balm for the soul, I hoped there would be young players trying to eke out a living by hurling and hitting a small spherical object – a cherry-coloured one – over an extended period of time.

I valued time with my therapist – even if I couldn't say I enjoyed it – to dig deep into the root of the triggered trauma that turned my grief into an insanity of some sort. And to discover how to cope with it. I was grateful, too, for the company and comfort of friends, both Vikki's and my own, who alternated between smoothing my path and dragging me through the obstacles on it. As a third element to my process, it was cricket that offered me a cocoon to absorb it all, to face or escape as the mood and circumstances took me.

Social media is often blamed, with good reason, for bile and nastiness that can damage one's mental health, but I was fortunate to find friends on Facebook who were understatedly supportive, and strangers on Twitter who were kind when they had no need to be. In a year, there was just one troll, who basically told me to shut up and man up. Personally, I think sharing pain is exactly what men need to do. I began to follow on Twitter several people who had also lost their wives and who regularly shared their experiences. They were a great help. One posted a diagram (*opposite*) that resonated.

At the time I first saw it, I doubted if I would ever feel the way they illustrated, but now it was beginning to make sense. At first, the ball of grief was huge and kept hitting the pain button every few minutes. Then the ball gradually grew smaller as it wore down. It still hit the pain button but less frequently. The ball still felt huge on some days, though, and when it did hit it could still be excruciating.

The process is, of course, going to be different for different people. I think the only direct advice I can offer anybody is to find "their cricket", whatever that might be, something to which they can latch on as both focus and diversion for grief. I found it at times hard to summon energy for activity, and would now and then even mean to set off for cricket before realising I just

Grief
(or the box and the ball)

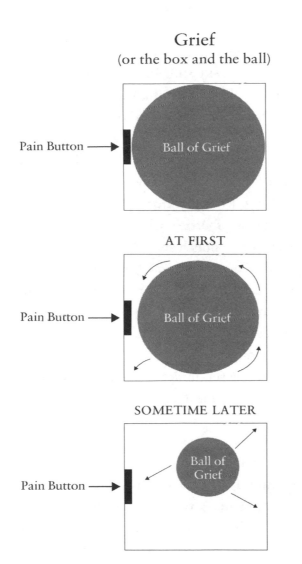

couldn't, but an interest that fits one's personality does feel essential.

And, if at all possible, find a good counsellor with whom to spill the unalloyed yucky stuff in confidence. "Grief," Bruce said to me, "will heal itself if it has support." I was beyond lucky to have him, but I also took advantage of the local hospice offering several sessions with a "listener", who was a sympathetic, empathetic ear. I could also be honest with good friends, in Alcoholics Anonymous too, notably Tony Adams. I was a patron of his mental health and addiction charity, Sporting Chance, and had even attended, a couple of months before Vikki died, a couple of his educational talks to county cricket clubs.

I will also be grateful, too, to the person who said the best, and most honest, thing that anybody could say to me when I was in a very dark moment. "Sometimes," she said, "there is no consolation." It immediately lifted the pressure on me – some self-inflicted – to feel I should be doing better, and helped me accept that this was simply, excruciatingly, painful.

As for the anxious agitation of it all, just recognising that it may strike, taking away the fear of the unknown, can dilute its power. It's a little like Yossarian in Joseph Heller's *Catch 22*: he knew that you have to be mad to get out of bombing missions, but to suggest to the doctor that you might be going mad shows you aren't.

Personal trauma – those painful episodes from the past that haunt us – will find any weak spot in those who grieve, I came to discover. And there are many weak spots. My experience was that – once I had become vulnerable through emotional pain – trauma and its bedfellow shame would find a way to burrow into the soul. I believed that one of the lessons for me, though, and one I could pass on, was that forewarned of that, of the potential for insanity, meant to be forearmed.

It took more than a year for something else to dawn on me and it took Bruce to point it out. I continued to struggle at weekends and Bruce noted that it had been on Saturdays and Sundays growing up when I had been at my most fearful due to the chaos and abandonment – the lack of availability of, and the need to reconnect with, those closest to me – to which I would often be subjected by the circumstances of our household. I don't know why I hadn't seen the link before between the grown man walking a tightrope and the kid walking on eggshells but I guess we learn lessons when we are ready. The realisation certainly lessened the anxiety's power over me gradually.

Bruce also introduced into my thinking the concept of the bardo, to help me with the process of letting go. It is, he told me, a state between death and rebirth in new life form that branches of Buddhism believe in. It requires the grieving eventually to let go of the loved one so that they will be free to continue their journey. It was not my belief but the concept intrigued me and if it did exist, I didn't want to deny Vikki her next destiny.

I recall saying to Bruce that I could, would never let Vikki go. Then I had a dream a couple of nights before the anniversary of her funeral. She was prone, looking up at me. "Don't do this," she was pleading. Some time later, I would have another dream in which she was welcoming me with open arms and we hugged and kissed. In the next scene, she was growing annoyed with me as I was talking when she wanted to watch TV. Our relationship in a nutshell. I awoke, desperate to get back the dream but it – she – was gone.

As I write this, I realise I feel some embarrassment both at this level of disclosure and some of my behaviour in the first year after Vikki's death. Looking back now, my jealousy over Vikki's previous lives, liaisons and relationships sounds silly; childish even. It is the shame of acquired trauma speaking, the pain of the child that echoes down the years. It tells someone like me that I should shut up and endure, rather than share. That no one will want to hear it. Should I bleed again in public? Risk being ridiculed? It seems I still do not trust my own instincts, do not believe I have something worthwhile to say that might both honour Vikki and help others.

That song by James, "Sit Down", echoes again here. As well as urging those who feel the breath of sadness to join them, the lyric also invites those who feel ridiculous. I, for one, often feel both.

While I began this book because I felt compelled to, I think I know now why I carried on and finished it, way beyond any personal catharsis it might have brought. For while my trauma, my jealousy and my fears might indeed seem ridiculous to the odd troll who thinks I should pull myself together and stop feeling sorry for myself (would that it were just that simple), there are many more people who will also have their own set of issues and feelings that may not resonate with me, as mine don't with them, but nevertheless are valid, and need acknowledging and airing, for their own well-being too. Unaddressed, they dog lives to the grave. As Toni Morrison said: "You wanna fly, you gotta give up the shit that weighs you down."

Vikki had fears and insecurities relating to abandonment, too; it was why we were trauma-bonded and could clash. Probably why it took us so long to get our act together and why, in that modern phrase, we could be co-dependent. But we persisted and were rewarded with a relationship in which we both felt alive, even if at times its volatility could be alarming. She didn't die wondering about whether we should have been together and I won't either.

Physically, the cancer that had spread in more of my pelvic lymph nodes in the months after Vikki's death was stabilised by a new drug for a year. Then, a blood test showed it had stopped working and the time for chemotherapy was approaching. "I'm working on five years," I said to the consultant when she told me that they might soon need to scan me and switch treatments. "That sounds realistic," she replied.

It struck me how bizarre things had become. I did not know where the time had gone. Sometimes, I was still stunned by a perceived unreality when I actually stopped to think that Vikki was, is, no longer here; at other times it was only too real and I acknowledged that stark reality. I had learned so much, accumulated knowledge, perhaps even some wisdom. And ain't it just the way that – prematurely in Vikki's, possibly within a few years of writing this in my case – life ends just when you think you have some kind of handle on it, have relaxed into it.

I thought of the 43-year-old Darren Stevens, the Kent all-rounder, who was being released by the county until in late season he made a superb career-best of 237 against Yorkshire then took 10 wickets in a match against Northamptonshire, prompting the offer of a new one-year contract. I hoped that I now had a last hurrah left in me. That was certainly a change for the better from being ready to turn down cancer treatment. In taking it, I was acknowledging Vikki's influence for good.

We all lose loved ones and I know my story is not unique. As I sat at The Oval during the final week of the season, I realised in the aloneness of the crowd that I was among people who all had their own tales to tell. As the saying had it, everyone is fighting a battle we know nothing about. So be kind. Sage, if not always – let's be honest – realistic.

I came to see that I was luckier than the majority who had lost their partner. Or had never had that special one person to grieve over. I acknowledged now the admiration and envy of those who saw what Vikki and I had and urged me to treasure the memories. And I had had the reflected splendour – though draining at times when in it, comforting afterwards – by association with a woman who was honoured so widely.

If, through nostalgia, I have idealised her and our relationship then I apologise, not least to her. She always wanted me to be real about her and us. In her office after her death, I found an account of her being diagnosed with cancer. She talked of her illness, of us and what we went through together, in fear and anger, with candour. But whatever its flaws, ours was a partnership of love and passion, of shared emotional intensity. Cancer robbed us of much physically but it could never dissipate that.

I do not believe my grieving has passed. Actually, though I sometimes worry about becoming a "grief bore" or remaining in what Graham Swift described as "unrelenting bereavement", I never want it to. My balance is fragile, fear of returning to the March madness capable of tipping me over. Sometimes, too, I fear I can't remember her properly; her expressions, her voice, her smell. Even what she looked like and how she moved. It prompts anxiety. I hate that I may be losing even her memory. But then I recall that these days I can picture her better when she was healthy, when we both were, and on top of our respective games. The effects of cancer, vivid still in the months after her death, robbed me of that for sad, angry periods. But death does not end love. If anything, it increases it.

Some say that the second year of grieving can be worse. The "firsts" may be over, all the anniversaries, but that leaves just a nothingness, I have been told. Nothing to celebrate, nothing to mark. Just her "goneness" is left. Perhaps. In Vikki's case, I suspected that the public recognition would dissolve, quite naturally. Simon Thomas said that he noticed that anything he posted on social media about his late wife and his and his son's grief would receive less of a reaction as time passed. I sensed, as did he, that people inevitably grow out of your pain and sadness, and that is understandable. They also, sensibly, leave you be to allow you gradually to stand on your own two feet.

Maybe it would indeed get tougher, though personally, I couldn't see how it could get any worse than those nights I would lie weeping on the landing in the darkness, shouting into her office, begging her to appear in some form that I could see, if only just once more.

But if that second year is to be worse than my first twelve months of living with pain and panic after the death of poor Vikki – poor, given the length of her years though certainly not the quality of them; hers was a dashing innings rather than a ground-out half-century – then at least for now allow me, as I need to allow myself, to feel grateful for having survived the bleakest year of my life and emerging to feel proud that Vikki was my wife, that she chose to share her remarkable life with me. That I wasn't meant to be there during her twenties, my thirties, as we might not have fitted together then as we later did. Ultimately, I was meant to be the one who stuck with her through her illness, as she did through mine. I was the one meant to kiss her forehead as she slipped away, meant to be the lasting element of her story and to tell it, to endure its aftermath and pass on its legacy.

Permit me to give myself a pat on the back for having at least occupied the crease in the face of some hostile bowling without giving my wicket away cheaply. Permit me too, just for now, the satisfaction of "having written".

Appendices

i. Vikki's final message

Written a week before she died, and delivered by Ian at Vikki's funeral, at her request

So Ian thought he had the last word... actually he finally will as he gets his turn in a few minutes.

It's slightly surreal planning your own funeral – and your own mother's too. I did worry at one point they would get muddled up. Given her musical taste differs somewhat from mine, if you suddenly hear the strains of a Shirley Bassey song coming down the aisle then something has gone wrong! Still, the control freak in me did at least get a say in the arrangements.

But it's also the first time I've not had to worry about numbers for a wedding or a Book Festival – have we sold enough tickets? (the Book Festival not the wedding!) Does the author like my interview? Why isn't that microphone working? Is the audience still awake?

If anyone *has* turned up, then thank you. I've asked Ian not to hold back in his eulogy as I know I sometimes didn't suffer fools gladly.

I think *Private Eye*'s Street of Shame – a rite of passage in any journalist's career – once described me as "feisty" and "shirty". Well, no excuses, but it was only because I cared. Thanks though to those who stuck with me along the way.

I've had the most amazing life and being first diagnosed 12 years ago tends to focus your priorities, so I was able to pack in trips to weird and wonderful places both through work and on holidays.

At my age you don't expect to make new friends either (as the cheery Sir Alex Ferguson once famously said, you only need six friends to carry your coffin) but I have – both up a mountain in Bhutan and in this beautiful village I moved to 14 years ago.

My initial target workwise was to reach London 2012. Well, I managed one more Olympics and, let's face it, Rio with gunshot sounds in the background was a survival test itself. In fact there were two Olympics without cancer and three with – not a bad statistic.

I know I've also not always done things the conventional way – though my stepdaughter Alex has helped compensate for that – and when your father takes you as a kid to football in the 1970s and doesn't bat an eyelid when you tell him you want to be a football writer, actively encouraging you to write for the fanzine, you suspect little is going to be conventional about your life.

Sheffield United, though, I fear are going to bottle it again. A whiff of automatic promotion and they crumble...

On that note, we don't want people to be sad today. The choice of music later might highlight this, and what happens now is another adventure, another country to visit, a test of trust and hope.

So please try and remember the good things. And good things in your life too.

As for that offside rule... I'm still working on it!

ii. Ian's eulogy

So, follow that... Vikki was a terrific writer, given her chance. A mistress of incisive brevity. I hope you'll forgive me if I go a tad over the word count on today of all days, though. Such a life, such a story, deserves justice and detail.

First, I want to thank you all for coming today. There are family and friends, people from sport and the media, from her beloved village and from afar. It is testament to her standing in both her professional and personal lives and the love, respect and admiration for her.

She would have approved, I hope, of all the *Sun* sports reporters being seated in the choir stalls.

As you have just heard, Vikki asked me to be honest about her. And as you've also heard, she had a fair degree of self-awareness. She kept, for example, an old *Peanuts* cartoon on our kitchen cork board. In it, Snoopy was sitting on top of his kennel at his typewriter. Vikki's alter-ego, Lucy, is telling Snoopy that he should write a novel about her life. He begins to type. "Born Crabby," he starts.

We will all have our memories, our pictures, of her. She meant many things to all of you here. The words pioneer and trailblazer have been justly used and it is so gratifying and comforting that her legacy will endure, which is pretty much all any of us can ask for. She was clearly a generous colleague, loyal friend, caring family member.

These will be my snapshots, as her husband, and they will stay with me for ever in my mind's eye. They amount not so much to an obituary. Amid all the overwhelming and unexpected but comforting media coverage, she would have found it funny that I even got scooped on that. I just want you to know her endearing essence. It is the story of us as much as the story of her, from one who knew her intimately and loved her deeply, shocking bunions and all.

Vikki Michelle Orvice – yes, she would roll her eyes at the *'Allo, 'Allo* link – was born in Sheffield in 1962 of good working-class stock. A proud Yorkshire woman, her character was forged in the Steel City.

Dad Fred was a mining engineer, Mum Jean a sales assistant in a department store. Vikki would be an only child, one taken to beautiful downtown Bramall Lane by Fred to foster a lifelong pessimism about Sheffield United. And a love for football in general. At the age of 12, she developed a lifelong crush on Johan Cruyff and a fondness for the colour orange.

Her favourite United player – and it is wonderful that he is here today, representing the club – was Tony Currie. I am well aware that the only reason Vikki married me was because TC never asked her. Tony, thank you for leaving the field clear.

She attended Westfield School at Mosborough, bright as a button academically, and was a Saturday girl at Asda in Orgreave.

The obits in *The Times* and *Telegraph* – and she would have smiled at being in the latter – have told the subsequent story. English at Leicester University, journalism college at Sheffield, indentures on the *Wakefield Express*, where she tried so hard but often failed to say nice things about local amateur dramatics. Rising to news editor at the *Western Daily Press* in Bristol.

Shifts on *The Observer*, where they seemed impressed that she actually knew how to pick up a phone and ring people for comment, and at the *Daily Mail*, where they soon offered her a staff job and where she became consumer affairs correspondent.

Then the desire to write about football full-time, an ambition fulfilled thanks to a brave sports editor in Paul Ridley, who made her the first woman sports staffer on a tabloid.

Years later, Paul would tell her that he thought she was "difficult". But he quickly added: "I like difficult. They make the best reporters."

At first, she worried she had made the wrong decision, found the going tough, the hoops narrower for a woman. The colleague who reckoned they'd have her out of there inside a week didn't know Vikki. How wrong can you be? Well, 24 years wrong.

Football was her first love, but track and field became her lasting passion when Paul raised the bar in 2000 and made her the paper's athletics correspondent, sending her to her first Olympics, in Sydney in 2000.

She phoned me from the stadium on the first athletics night, excited but concerned that she would not do justice to herself and the event and let the paper down, knowing that she had the big shoes of the legendary Colin Hart to fill. "Big players rise to big occasions," I said. She liked that, thanked me. And she became a big player that night.

Vikki was there that day in Singapore 2005 when London was awarded the 2012 Games, delighted for her friend and fellow Sheffield alumnus, Sebastian Coe, the local boy's golden exploits inspiring her love of the sport when she was growing up.

She would value deeply Lord Coe's consequent friendship, treasured the personal note of thanks for her role in getting *The Sun* to back the campaign, knowing how valuable their support could be. Cannily, she knew too she would have a contact on the inside.

When Vikki was diagnosed with her cancer in 2007, she asked the amazing Professor Ian Smith at the Royal Marsden Hospital to keep her alive to cover London. My personal thanks to him, and all his team at the Marsden too, for extending that by almost seven years.

(You know, oncologists and Marsden staff do not go to funerals. As you can imagine, the pain and regularity would be too draining. Three of the great team who kept her going for so long are here today, however, such an impression did Vikki make.)

Vikki took great pride in carrying the Olympic torch in South Yorkshire in the run-up to the 2012

Games; always cited Super Saturday as the finest night of her career. And it gladdened her dying heart in recent months that the three gold medallists – Greg Rutherford, Mo Farah and Jess Ennis – all sent her videos and text messages of support, along with that athlete she was most grateful to for her trips around the world, Paula Radcliffe.

(Jess, incidentally, sent a follow-up text saying: "It's Jess Ennis-Hill, in case you were wondering which Jess it was.")

Vikki loved athletes, their travails and their triumphs, in such a lonely sport. And she adored their down-to-earth nature that matched hers.

Her relationships with them were those of a specialist who knew her subject and made lasting contacts. They trusted her. They gave her exclusives. All because of the leg work she put in. Often she would go to events that would make little or no copy, simply to say hello, foster contacts, get phone numbers for those times when there would be a story.

Rio was a bonus, Tokyo a Games too far, but she ran a great race for the sport and deserves her podium place. The forthcoming European Indoor Championships in Glasgow will have the Vikki Orvice Media Centre to serve it. So too the London Marathon in April in another remarkable tribute to her. I hope both will have logos of sharp elbows rampant. She reckoned they were the sharpest in any mixed zone.

All the while, Vikki devoted herself to making sports journalism better, particularly for women. She was the first woman chair of the British Athletics Writers Association, and she hated me at functions introducing myself to people with "Hello, I'm Denis Thatcher."

She was rightly proud of being the first non-athlete to receive the organisation's Inspiration Award in 2016. She sat also on the media committee of the International Athletics Federation. In addition, she was vice-chair of the Football Writers Association and served on the committee of the Sports Journalists Association.

Above all, Vikki was delighted to be on the board of Women In Football from the early days, helping it grow from a few disaffected souls sharing injustices into the hugely influential organisation it is today. There, she found sistership and support, loved to receive it, loved more to give it back to younger women in need of help up the greasy pole.

Indeed, her championing of women in the media was inspirational, to the point shortly before her death, she asked *The Sun* to establish a scholarship for an aspiring woman sports journalist. All credit to her sports editor Shaun Custis and the paper for having already launched the initiative.

Vikki did not always agree with *The Sun*'s take on life – what journalist does with their paper? – but she was fiercely loyal and loved it when it held power to account and sided with the underdog.

At one point, she was on a trial drug at the Marsden – where she somehow also found time to be a patient governor on the board for six years – called Palbociclib and it worked for around 26 marvellous months. She wanted others to have it too and joined the campaign to get the drug made widely available. *The Sun* gave her space on the news pages to write about it and Palbociclib would soon be sanctioned by the National Institute for Health Care and Excellence.

(At this point I think Vikki would want me to say it: there is such power for good in a modern written press that can, with reason at times, be derided. But we stop paying for journalism by those who are trained and have accumulated experience and contacts at our peril. And while I'm at it, let me say on behalf of Vikki: guys, give a gal a break. There's room for everyone. Success is not finite. It expands.)

What of those rare hours when she wasn't busy? Vikki loved books and reading, loved the arts indeed, be it paintings, the theatre, cinema, concerts classical and modern. I thank her for civilising me, for introducing and taking me to so much. Apart from some dreadful turkeys at The Donmar.

With Mark and Mary Jenkin, she established the Flamstead Book Festival in aid of this beautiful church, the place in which we were married and which she loved so much. She booked some remarkable names, including Sarah Vaughan, Sophie Hannah, Barry Norman and Tony Parsons.

As you can see, Vikki had her finger in so many pies. Unfortunately, that left her with no time to make any. Luckily, as she noted, a divorce from my first wife taught me how to cook. Her contempt for an ironing board, meanwhile, was matched only by that for obstructive press officers.

What else? She loved to travel, and made it to five continents. She always found the best little hotels and restaurants. In the heart of Venice on our honeymoon, she even found one with a garden. Just before her death, she lamented to me that she had never made it to Namibia and Easter Island. "If those are the only two places you're worried about not visiting, Vikki, you haven't done too badly," I said.

So those are the signposts of her life. In reaching each one there was character, drive, persistence, talent and tenacity in abundance. And yes, stubbornness. No defect that, though, when you have cancer. It kept her alive for so long.

Once, by the way, we were sitting next to Sir Bobby Robson at a Football Writers' Dinner. "Vikki has cancer as well," I said to Bobby. "What type?" he asked her. "Well, they think the primary was breast but it could have been ovarian," she replied. "Them, pet," he said, "are the only two I've not had."

How else to describe her? Sweet, demur, conciliatory... Those are just some of the descriptions that Vikki would hate me to use about her. There is a Sheffield word that works well: mardy. But then, I have to admit, I could match her for mardiness on my day.

The tensions of cancer take their toll. Though she never wanted to be seen as brave, she was undoubtedly enviably stoical in her last months. She had an arrangement with it: if you don't get uppity, she would say to it, we can live together. Sadly there are only so many times you can ask a scorpion not to sting.

She was also competitive. She wanted us to write a book together called "My cancer's worse than yours". Sadly, too, she was right about that. She always was. Even when she was wrong.

So yes, we had our ups and downs, as those who knew us well would testify. But they came too with love, passion, a shared sense of humour and cultural interests. Anyway, ups and downs are the rhythm of life. Like the movements on a cardiograph, they show you're alive. And how alive Vikki was.

She was gregarious, tender, vulnerable, warm-hearted and funny, with a smile as wide as the M1 at Tinsley Viaduct. She was waspishly witty and I wasn't spared. When I came home from the British Press Awards with the Sports Journalist of the Year trophy 12 years ago, she was in bed and looked up from her book to say: "I told you it was a Zara Phillips kind of year."

So farewell, my lovely. I'll be seeing you in all the old familiar places... The members terrace at Tate Modern, the foyer of the National Theatre, the pier at Southwold in your Jackie O sunglasses. In King's College Chapel in Cambridge at evensong or *When Some Like It Hot* is on at the Rex.

I'll be hearing you, in the piano of Keith Jarrett and voice of Van Morrison, on Radio 4 Sunday mornings and via the commentaries of Mike Costello and the pre-senting of Jacqui Oatley. Reading you in the poetry of Julia Darling and the prose of Dorothy Parker. Tasting you in the linguine vongole on the seafront at Camogli.

Yours was not a long life, but better one short and broad – of mind, achievement and adventure – rather than long and narrow.

Goodnight, my Saturday girl.

iii. Vikki's Obituary in The Times

Register

Vikki Orvice

Pioneering sports journalist who confronted male

While reporting on the England Under-21 men's football team in Cyprus, Vikki Orvice was once asked by the head of its football association why she wasn't "at home making beautiful things". Later, she was asked by a press room steward at a match if she thought they had made enough sandwiches for the male writers.

As a sports reporter with *The Sun*, Orvice was the first woman to be appointed as a football writer on a redtop tabloid. When she was offered the job in 1995 the sports editor, Paul Ridley, felt he had to defend her by saying: "She's here because she's good. Not because she's a woman."

Made of something akin to steel and with a work ethic to match, Orvice recalled: "Some managers were inappropriate in postmatch interviews but my colleagues — once I had convinced them that I knew my stuff and was there for the longhaul — slowly began to support me."

Orvice became part of a small group of women who were fed up with being overlooked or excluded — including Shelley Alexander, now with the BBC — which became the Women In Football network. They would meet at Pizza Express in Soho to share stories about prejudicial treatment, such as not being given the same access to players as male journalists, and would take up the issues with the relevant football authorities. She later became a director of the organisation.

Over the years, through the good old-fashioned nurturing of contacts, she wrote a number of exclusives, including interviews with the athletes Mo Farah, Paula Radcliffe and Jessica Ennis-Hill. She particularly enjoyed sharing a taxi with Usain Bolt to the Olympic Stadium in London, which was still being built, for an interview. When there was criticism to be

dished out — of individuals or a sport — she never ducked the issues. Indeed, she was held in such respect that the IAAF, the governing body of athletics, would often use her as a sounding board on behalf of the global media.

Her energy was prodigious. She planned each assignment and often confronted editors who, in her opinion, did not do her stories justice. According to one colleague who was with her in Rio de Janeiro for the 2016 Olympics, "She was a human whirlwind, crisscrossing a huge, steaming-hot city to cover this event and that, filing reams of copy every day, organising everyone around her, first down for breakfast in the morning and the last to turn in."

She worked 16 hours a day, seven days a week, from the first drum-beat of the opening ceremony to the final firework of the closing show. And she did it all while living with terminal cancer, dismissing advice that she should not expose herself to the zika virus.

Back in Britain, she continued to work while having treatment and hated to miss a single event. "I've been to every Olympics since Sydney, World Cup finals and Wimbledon," she wrote shortly before her death, "I've watched every one of Usain Bolt's record-breaking races."

She also joked that "covering a midweek match in December in Stoke, and crossing some waste ground at midnight to get to my iced-up car, is an excellent reality check".

Vikki Michelle Orvice was born in 1962 and grew up in Sheffield. An only child, she was taken to Sheffield United at a young age by her father, Fred, who was a mining engineer. Her mother, Jean, worked as a shop assistant at a department store in Mansfield.

As a young girl she entered a match report for a *Daily Express* sports writing competition. "I loved Holland's

(Reprinted with kind permission of *The Times*)

chauvinism in football and worked relentlessly through her illness

EDDIE KEOGH/THE SUN; JIM KEOGH

Vikki Orvice interviewing David Beckham in 1998 and, left, with the Great Britain sailor Steve Mitchell in 2004. She covered every Olympics since Sydney in 2000

Johan Cruyff and the Sheffield United player Tony Currie, a maverick who blew kisses to the crowd," Orvice recalled. There were few women role models, however.

She was asked if there were enough sandwiches for the male reporters

Later, she developed a love of athletics while following the feats of her fellow Sheffielder Seb Coe, who became a friend. At the The Sun she championed the campaign Lord Coe led for London to host the Games.

She had always wanted to be a sports journalist and never thought that gender would be a barrier — until she tried. After graduating with a degree in English from the University of Leicester, she took a trainee course in journalism in Sheffield. On one occasion she submitted a match report for a project and was told it was "very good", before being asked if it had been written by her boyfriend.

She started work as a reporter on the Wakefield Express, covering local councils and reviewing plays in Leeds. She won a Yorkshire journalism award for an interview with Enid Hattersley, Roy's mother who had been Lord Mayor of Sheffield in 1981.

Later, she moved to the Western Daily Press in Bristol where she became news editor. She started doing shifts on The Observer and the Daily Mail, who recognised her diligence and gave her a staff job as consumer affairs corre-

spondent. She asked to cover football matches and the Mail agreed, but told her it would not lead to a staff job on the sports desk.

After joining The Sun, Orvice wrote about football for seven years, then covered her first Olympics, Sydney 2000, where Cathy Freeman, an athlete of aboriginal descent, set the host nation alight by winning gold in the 400m. Orvice loved it. In 2002 she became athletics correspondent. Her favourite Olympic moment was "Super Saturday" at London 2012 when Ennis-Hill, Farah and Greg Rutherford all won gold for Team GB.

In 2010 she married Ian Ridley, a fellow sportswriter, who survives her. She had a stepdaughter, Alex, who is a picture editor and photographer, and a stepson, Jack, who is a musician and songwriter. They lived in the village of Flamstead in Hertfordshire.

A joyous woman who loved reading, especially novels, she co-founded her village book festival and secured speakers such as the broadcaster and author Tony Parsons. She was a member of the Tate, enjoyed plays at the National Theatre and in the West End, and concerts at the Royal Festival Hall.

After she had breast cancer diagnosed in early 2007 she became a tireless campaigner and advocate for the Royal Marsden cancer hospital. She wrote about a new drug called Palbociclib, which helped to extend her own life for two years, and played a part in convincing the National Institute of Clinical Excellence to make it more widely available. While she was under treatment, she was delighted to receive a video message from Farah and Rutherford — "That's pretty special."

After her death, The Sun announced that it would launch a Vikki Orvice memorial sports journalism scholarship in her honour. In 2018, she had written an article reflecting on her career to mark The Sun's 50th anniversary later this year. "Not a bad innings," she concluded, "for someone who was not supposed to last a week!"

Vikki Orvice, sports reporter, was born on November 8, 1962. She died of cancer on February 6, 2019, aged 56

iv. Vikki's final piece

By VIKKI ORVICE
Trailblazing *SunSport* writer 1995–2019

A FEMALE ON SPORT? ONLY AT THE SUN ...

THE *Daily Mail*'s Sports Editor was clear: 'I don't think a woman can write about football full-time.' It was after August 1992, the launch of the Premier League, when I started covering matches at the *Mail* on top of my job as a news reporter. But there was no place for a woman as a staff sports writer.

In 1995 *The Sun*'s Sports Editor, Paul Ridley, offered me a job as the first female football staff writer on a tabloid. I had dreamed of covering football. My dad was a Sheffield United fan and had taken me to matches since I was three. I loved Holland's Johan Cruyff and Sheffield United player Tony Currie, a maverick who blew kisses to the crowd.

Female role models back then were non-existent – Julie Welch a lone figure blazing a trail on the broadsheets – so I took the news route through local papers. But I loved covering matches.

Paul told me *The Sun* had the best sports team but what they didn't have was a woman. He was brave – I was joining THE football paper from just doing match reports part-time.

Some colleagues predicted I wouldn't last a week. There was a lot of pressure to make the unusual appointment work. I remember Paul yelling down the phone after another request to interview me on radio or TV: 'It's no freak show, she's here on merit!'

That first week I reported from Cardiff and Millwall. Surviving matches there meant you could survive anything. Some managers were inappropriate in post-match interviews but my colleagues – once I had convinced them I knew my stuff and was there for the long haul – slowly began to support me. The players would often open up to me.

I started covering athletics in 2000 and later tennis. I've been to every Olympics since Sydney, World Cup finals and Wimbledon. I've watched all Usain Bolt's record-breaking races.

But covering a midweek December match in Stoke and crossing waste ground at midnight to get to my iced-up car is an excellent reality check. Building contacts takes years of attending those matches and waiting to talk to players.

I have had cancer, and Mo Farah and Greg Rutherford filmed a get well message for me. That's pretty special.

The Sun has had so much stick about Page 3 but no one remembers they were actively seeking female sports reporters 24 years ago. I'm still there. Not bad for someone who wasn't supposed to last a week.

Vikki Orvice died on 6 February 2019, aged 56

(Reprinted with kind permission of *The Sun*)

Acknowledgements

· ·

Those who supported me in the wake of Vikki's death are many and their roles, I hope, are given due credit in the narrative. Some do need special, additional mention. Above all I am intensely indebted to Bruce Lloyd, who continues to save my life on a weekly basis, and my children Alex and Jack.

Those I would most like to thank for their practical and moral support in our village are the selfless Moira Thoubboron, Jackie and Richard Scopes, Mark and Mary Jenkin, Mark Evans and the Rev. Tom Sander.

Then my and Vikki's great friends: Janet King, Paul Crosbie, Liz Sparke, Tom Knight and Sybil Ruscoe, Emma and Richard Visick, Shirley Clift and Jeroen Knops, along with Vikki's cousins Lee Stansfield and Lyn Reeves.

Thanks to my male friends who were generous with their sharing and listening: Jimmy Mulville, Tony Adams, Ian Chapman, Darren Barker, Simon Thomas, Mike McMonagle and Steve Claridge. Keith Blackmore and Paul Hayward were perceptive, encouraging guides on the book itself.

My gratitude also to the women who offered kind and wise words: Rosemary Clough, Denise O'Donoghue, Serena Bird, Jacqui Barker, Daniela Sieff, Jayne Pearce-McMenamin, Amanda Smith, Amanda Newbery, Kate Battersby and Tracey Ann Morton.

So many people loved Vikki and I will be forever grateful to Jacqui Oatley, Jo Tongue, Carrie Brown, Jane Purdon, Anna Kessel and Sarah Shephard, along with Philippe Auclair, Mike Collett and Gerry Cox, for sharing that love with me.

My thanks for their generosity, too, to *Tortoise* news website, News UK, Sheffield United and Arsenal football clubs, and to the wonderful Royal Marsden Hospital, especially the sensitive Kaz Mochlinski, and its charity arm. I also appreciate Michael Atherton OBE and Julia Samuel MBE reading and reviewing the manuscript so kindly.

At Floodlit Dreams, we have developed into something of a family and Seth Burkett and Susie Petruccelli have been great supports. Thanks also to the talented Steve Leard for his cover design. Special gratitude goes to my brilliant editor Charlotte Atyeo, who "got" this book and sprinkled it with a delicate and perceptive empathy.

Finally, I will forever be in the debt of someone without whom nothing would have been possible these past 31 years, Bill W.

Ian Ridley, May 2020

ALSO BY IAN RIDLEY

Sports Books

SEASON IN THE COLD
A Journey Through English Football

CANTONA
The Red and the Black

TALES FROM THE BOOT CAMPS
with Steve Claridge

ADDICTED
with Tony Adams

HERO AND VILLAIN
with Paul Merson

FLOODLIT DREAMS
How to Save a Football Club

KEVIN KEEGAN
An Intimate Portrait of Football's Last Romantic

BEYOND THE BOOT CAMPS
with Steve Claridge

THERE'S A GOLDEN SKY
How Twenty Years of the Premier League
Changed Football Forever

ADDED TIME
Surviving Cancer, Death Threats and the Premier League
with Mark Halsey

A DAZZLING DARKNESS
The Darren Barker Story
with Darren Barker

SOBER
with Tony Adams

Novel

THE OUTER CIRCLE

ALSO BY FLOODLIT DREAMS

ADDED TIME
Surviving Cancer, Death Threats and the Premier League
By Mark Halsey with Ian Ridley

THE BOY IN BRAZIL
Living, Learning and Loving in the Land of Football
By Seth Burkett

A DAZZLING DARKNESS
The Darren Barker Story
By Darren Barker with Ian Ridley

THE SOCCER SYNDROME
English Football's Golden Age
By John Moynihan
(Foreword by Patrick Barclay)

THE HITLER TROPHY
Golf and the Olympic Games
By Alan Fraser

FOOTBALL'S COMING OUT
Life as a Gay Fan and Player
By Neil Beasley with Seth Burkett

RAISED A WARRIOR
One Woman's Soccer Odyssey
By Susie Petruccelli